- An understanding of the issues that come into play as you build your onshore or offshore fund, and as you prospect for assets
- Advice on developing marketing strategies that can help you accumulate capital for your fund
- The tools to establish an infrastructure that can effectively support your business

By showing you how to efficiently manage the business side of a hedge fund, this book will help you—and your partners—form a fund that will create and preserve wealth for you and your investors.

Filled with in-depth insights and real-world examples, *The Fundamentals of Hedge Fund Management* provides you with the tools and techniques necessary to successfully launch and operate a hedge fund in today's competitive marketplace.

DANIEL A. STRACHMAN is Managing Director of A & C Advisors LLC, a diversified investment management firm that offers services to individuals and institutions. Strachman is also the Editor of *The Strachman Report*, a bimonthly newsletter about long-term investment strategies. He has worked in product development, marketing, and sales focused around the money management industry. He is also author of *Getting Started in Hedge Funds, Essential Stock Picking Strategies,* and *Julian Robertson,* all of which are published by Wiley.

The Fundamentals of Hedge Fund Management

Founded in 1807, John Wiley & Sons is the oldest independent publishing company in the United States. With offices in North America, Europe, Australia, and Asia, Wiley is globally committed to developing and marketing print and electronic products and services for our customers' professional and personal knowledge and understanding.

The Wiley Finance series contains books written specifically for finance and investment professionals as well as sophisticated individual investors and their financial advisors. Book topics range from portfolio management to e-commerce, risk management, financial engineering, valuation, and financial instrument analysis, as well as much more.

For a list of available titles, please visit our Web site at www.Wiley Finance.com.

The Fundamentals of Hedge Fund Management

How to Successfully Launch and Operate a Hedge Fund

DANIEL A. STRACHMAN

John Wiley & Sons, Inc.

Published by John Wiley & Sons, Inc., Hoboken, New Jersey.
Published simultaneously in Canada.

For general information on our other products and services or for technical support, please contact our Customer Care Department within the United States at (800) 762–2974, outside the United States at (317) 572–3993 or fax (317) 572–4002.

Wiley also publishes its books in a variety of electronic formats. Some content that appears in print may not be available in electronic books. For more information about Wiley products, visit our Web site at www.wiley.com.

Library of Congress Cataloging-in-Publication Data

Strachman, Daniel A., 1971-
  The fundamentals of hedge fund management : how to successfully launch and operate a hedge fund / Daniel A. Strachman.
      p. cm.
  Includes bibliographical references and index.
  ISBN-13: 978–0–471–74852–6 (cloth)
  ISBN-10: 0–471–74852–8 (cloth)
  1. Hedge funds. I. Title.
  HG4530.S8368 2007
  332.64'5—dc22   2006015453

Printed in the United States of America

10 9 8 7 6 5 4

"The day is short; the task is great."

Ethics of the Fathers
Chapter II Verse 20

"Opportunity is missed by most people because it is dressed in overalls and looks like work."

Thomas A. Edison

To Felice, Leah, and Jonah

Contents

Preface

Over the past five years, the hedge fund industry has grown enormously. Hedge funds, which were once thought of as a tool of the rich and privileged, are commonplace in investment portfolios around the world. No matter what you read, see, or hear in the popular press, the hedge fund industry is here to stay. Even in the wake of the collapse of Amaranth Advisors, the industry is stronger than ever and has become a force to be reckoned with both here and abroad.

Now is a wonderful time to be entering the hedge fund industry, for a number of different reasons. First, the industry is primed for growth; second, the markets are extremely volatile; and third, hedge funds have come into their own, literally on someone else's nickel, which means a lot of the work you previously would have had to do to build your business has been done for you, and the road to hedge fund riches is going to be a lot smoother than it was, say, five or six years ago. However, that being said, building a successful business is going to take a lot of hard work; there are going to be a lot of disappointing times; and it is going to be extremely frustrating more often than not. Therefore, my advice is as follows: Be prepared for the worst, expect the best, and be satisfied on some level with your success.

I believe that the industry is primed for growth, and with this growth I believe there will be a lot of questions. The intention of this book is to answer some, if not all, of the questions that you or your colleagues may have and provide you with at least a foundation for your business and tools that will enable you to find the answers.

Over the past 10 years, I have had the unique experience of working literally around the world with people who are creating, building, developing, and marketing hedge funds. Some are just starting out and have less than $1 million in assets under management; some are well-heeled firms with billions in assets under management; others fall somewhere in between. While their situations are different and in some sense unique to them, they all have the same questions, they all need basically the same answers, and they don't have a place to turn to for advice. My job is to give them that advice, whether they want to hear it or not; my job is to tell it like it is and to help them get to where they need to be with their business.

During this time, I have worked with clients in 20 countries on four continents; it has been quite a wild ride. The key for me is to be able to solve problems for those in the hedge business who fly without a net because they are not part of some investment management behemoth.

This book provides you with some of what you need to be successful. It provides you with the tools you need to make good decisions, the tools you need to create good plans, the tools you need to set out a marketing strategy to help you raise assets, and the tools you need to create an infrastructure that will allow you to support your business.

Your goal in reading this book is to learn as much as you can about how to operate the business side of a hedge fund. This book is not about money management strategies. This book is not about buying low and selling high. It is about the infrastructure, the business side, of the hedge fund industry, and I believe that as you read the following pages, you will learn the fundamentals that you need to run a successful business.

This book will not solve all problems or provide you with everything you need to be successful; it will give you the fundamentals. One thing you should also look for as you go out on your own is a mentor. In order to be successful, you need good, solid advice givers, and you need to be willing to take advice and look for it. Don't be embarrassed or too proud to ask for help. It is okay to have questions—the key is finding answers.

This book that you have purchased should be viewed as a great resource tool. It should be something that you use time and time again to help you understand, deal with, and operate your business more efficiently and successfully. I hope you will get as much joy from reading and rereading it as I have from writing it. As I say more than once throughout these pages, if you have any questions about anything that you read in this book, or if you have issues you want to discuss, you can always send me an e-mail at das@hedgeanswers.com.

Thanks for purchasing this book. I hope you enjoy it.

Acknowledgments

The idea for this book came about through a series of e-mails between my editor and me during the last few weeks of 2004. Since that time, I have spent an enormous amount of time trying to figure out what makes a hedge fund successful and what causes a hedge fund to fail. And although I have yet to find empirical evidence that defines success and failure, I believe that, in the pages that follow, I have provided you with a road map that will allow you to avoid failure and to succeed. Your interest in hedge funds has made this book possible. I thank you very much for your interest in this fascinating subject.

I wrote the second edition of *Getting Started in Hedge Funds* because these unique investment products are here to stay. They are no longer considered an "alternative" investment vehicle, but rather an important part of a diversified portfolio. And, while hedge funds have not yet become "traditional," in the months and years ahead the characteristics that separate traditional investments and hedge funds are going to become smaller and smaller. Hedge funds are not going to disappear because people understand the value of creating a portfolio that is hedged against market volatility. Hedge funds are for investors of all shapes and sizes and play an important role in the future of the financial markets.

As in the past, to write this book I have called on many of the usual suspects who have helped me over the years look good in print. It has become more and more evident to me that there is nothing more important than to have good people at your side. These people are better than good, and without them I would not be able to get my work done. They are, of course, Viki Goldman, the greatest librarian and researcher I have ever met, and Sam Graff, the only true newspaper man left in the tristate area. Thank you for your hard work and for always making my work better. I truly appreciate everything you do for me. Special thanks also to Christine Enners, who came through with the logistical support to make this book a reality.

The people at Wiley have once again provided me a platform for my work. To all of them, I say thank you. I hope the book is all you intended it to be when you gave me the go-ahead to write it.

I want to thank my family for their support and guidance over the years. It is through your efforts that this book is possible.

And to my wife Felice, all I can say is thank you for being a provider of inspiration and support to see this and all of the other projects through from start to finish.

Daniel Strachman
Fanwood, New Jersey
November 2006

CHAPTER 1

The Hedge Fund Industry

The growth of the hedge fund industry over the past five years is truly amazing. Many industry observers believe that since the dawn of the new millennium, assets in these often-called secretive investment vehicles has grown fourfold. If you factor in the number of funds of funds, the growth factor is probably closer to fivefold. The industry continues to grow at a record pace, even with the weak performance numbers in 2005 and the decrease in asset inflows in the first quarter of 2006.

According to one published report, 2,073 hedge funds were launched in 2005, up from 1,435 in 2004.[1] As of spring 2006, there are an estimated 12,000 hedge funds in operation globally.[2] The numbers are shocking and quite compelling, especially if you are working at a service provider. Some in the industry equate the substantial growth in hedge funds over the past five years to what happened in the mutual fund industry in the late 1980s and early 1990s. The result was an industry that contracted in light of the bursting technology bubble and bear market. Many believe that as the hedge fund industry continues to grow, it is readying itself for a bursting, of sorts. Therefore, as the new manager on the block, you need to be ready for what lies ahead, because, quite frankly, it does not look so pretty. That being said, the strong will survive, and they will prosper. Your job as a new manager about to launch a fund is to make sure that you are ready, willing, and able to deal with everything that the market and investors throw at you and that you are prepared for the worst.

To understand where the industry is going, you need to first understand where it has been. The evolution of the hedge fund industry is best seen by coming out of the Wall Street subway stop. When you exit the station, head northwest toward Broadway and make a quick left on Broad Street: In front of you will be the New York Stock Exchange, behind you will be the former headquarters of J.P. Morgan, and to your left will be a statue of President George Washington.

If you make this trip around 9:00 A.M., you will see exactly what Alfred Winslow Jones saw—traders and brokers hustling to get inside the building before the market opens. It was the action and excitement of this place that led Jones to create the first known *hedged fund*, an investment vehicle that went long and short the market and was able to protect and grow its investors' assets regardless of market conditions.

Jones, a sociologist turned journalist, came up with the concept of this long/short fund based on a thesis he had written for an article in *Fortune* magazine.

In the late 1940s, Jones had held a number of positions in journalism, writing about finance and industry as well as social issues. During this time, he realized that the income he earned as a freelancer was not going to be enough to sustain him or his family in the life that he expected and wanted. He looked to Wall Street for the answer. What he found was an idea that he believed would work. In turn, he would earn enough money to support his family and to fulfill his major passion—helping people. While Jones clearly developed his concept and his business for the money it earned him, his idea was to take the wealth and put it to work in the community. His idea was to use his hedged fund as a tool for others to help themselves. His son-in-law, Robert Burch, who currently runs A.W. Jones & Company with his son, said that Jones was more interested in the intellectual challenge of the business than the rewards that it provided.

"Jones was not a man that was very interested in Wall Street," said Burch. "Although he made a lot of money over the years, he gave quite a lot of it away in order to create programs and organizations to help people here in the United States."

Jones was not interested in talking about the fund, how it worked, or what it did; he wanted to talk about how to make the country and the world a better place.

"When you had dinner with Jones, you always had four or five guys from various parts of the world," recalls Burch. "You didn't know if that night you were going to discuss some pending revolt in Albania or what language they speak in Iran. But what you did know was that you would definitely not be talking about money, Wall Street, or the firm. His mind was beyond that."

The foundation of the hedge fund industry lay not in the pursuit of money for conspicuous consumption but in the pursuit of money to help people.

It all began in a magazine. The article was not some how-to or get-rich-quick piece about making a fast buck, but rather a thought-provoking look at how money is managed and the idea that going long some stocks and short others can earn great and stable rewards. In short, the Jones piece looked at how you could go long a basket of stocks and short a basket of stocks and still protect and grow your assets.

The article that put his plan in motion was titled "Fashion in Forecasting," which ran in the March 1949 issue of *Fortune* magazine. It gave him the foundation for what today some people view as one of the most important tools used by money managers to actually make money. Following is an excerpt* from the article:

> *The standard, old-fashioned method of predicting the course of the stock market is first to look at facts and figures external to the market itself, and then examine stock prices to see whether they are too high or too low. Freight-car loadings, commodity prices, bank clearings, the outlook for tax legislation, political prospects, the danger of war, and countless other factors determine corporations' earnings and dividends, and these, combined with money rates, are supposed to (and in the long run do) determine the prices to common stocks. But in the meantime awkward things get in the way (and in the long run, as Keynes said, we shall be dead).*
>
> *In the late summer of 1946, for instance, the Dow Jones industrial stock average dropped in five weeks from 205 to 163, part of the move to a minor panic. In spite of the stock market, business was good before the break, remained good though it, and has been good ever since.*
>
> *Nevertheless there are market analysts, whose concern is the internal character of the market, who could see the decline coming. To get these predictive powers they study the statistics that the stock market itself grinds out day after day. Refined, manipulated in various ways, and interpreted, these data are sold by probably as many as twenty stock market services and are used independently by hundreds, perhaps thousands, of individuals. They are increasingly used by brokerage firms, by some because the users believe in them and by others because their use brings in business.*[3]

The idea was simple: Some stocks go up while others go down, and very rarely do all stocks move in the same direction at the same time. If this makes sense to you, then the next thing you need to understand is that as some stocks move up and others move down, there is a way to make money both when they go up, by being long a basket of stocks, and when they go down, by being short a basket of stocks. The key is to forecast which stocks go up and which go down and to position a portfolio accordingly.

---

*© 1949 Time Inc. All rights reserved.

The issue then was no different than the issue today: How do you de-termine which stocks are going to go up and which are going to go down? Jones had a unique problem. He was not a stock picker. Fortunately, he learned this early on and was able to compensate for his inability to pick stocks by hiring those who could.

"My father was a good salesman; he knew people to raise money from, and was a good organizer and administrator. But when it came to picking stocks, he had no particular talent," said Tony Jones. "This meant that his job was to find people who did have the talent."

Alfred Winslow Jones was an executive, not a stock picker. He under-stood how to get things done and how to find people to execute his ideas. In the end, he created the first hedge fund—and with it an entire industry.

Some 50-odd years later, in the fall of 2003, a report by the Securities and Exchange Commission estimated that there were 6,000 to 7,000 hedge funds managing between $600 billion to $650 billion in assets. The report noted that hedge fund assets were expected to grow to more than $1 tril-lion between 2008 and 2010.[4]

Jones never saw this coming. He believed that his business did not have legs, even though it was successful and even though his concept worked. In one of the few profiles of the founder of the hedge fund industry, Jones is quoted as saying, "I don't believe that it [the hedge fund] is ever going to become as big a part of the investment scene as it was in the 1960s. The hedge fund does not have a terrific future."[5]

Jones seemed to have misunderstood the value of his invention be-cause, as many people realize, having a portfolio that is both long and short is the only way over a long period of time to ensure that their assets are protected and grow regardless of whether the market rises or falls.

While a portfolio of longs and a portfolio of shorts make sense, the key to long-term success is not just to hit the ball out of the park with your stock picks but to put up singles and doubles each and every day. Move the runners around the bases and back to home plate while protecting your as-sets at all costs to make sure you live to fight another day. That, my friends, is the secret of successful hedge fund businesses, and it allows these organi-zations to maintain and create wealth in a safe and secure environment.

UNDERSTANDING HEDGE FUNDS

The idea of this book is simple. It provides you with the tools you need to understand the functions that go into creating, launching, and running an investment vehicle that is a hedge fund. It provides you with information to make better decisions when choosing a lawyer, prime broker, accountant, administrator, and other service providers—the people who will help you grow and maintain your business. It provides you with insight into the perceptions versus the realities of the hedge fund business. And most of all, it gives you a clear understanding of where the hedge fund industry came from, where it is now, and where it is going. In this way, you and your partners can create and run a successful business that allows you and your investors to build and preserve wealth.

This book is not about managing money or implementing trading strategies. That is covered in other, more thought-provoking books about money and markets. This book is a tool—a reference guide, if you will—that will be used by your front-, middle-, and back-office personnel. It will be used when you decide what sort of funds to launch, how they should be structured, who you should choose as a lawyer and prime broker, among others, and most important, who your funds can be marketed to. If you want to learn about trading, stop reading right now.

With that said, we now need to look at hedge fund basics in order to figure how to get started on developing and running a successful business. The basics are, quite honestly, very basic. One thing that needs to be said up front is that hedge funds, like most things on Wall Street, are thought to be very intricate, confusing, and sophisticated. This is just not the case. Hedge funds, like most everything else on the Street, are quite simple when you break them down and quite easy to understand once you look at them closely and dissect them in an orderly and efficient manner.

Some aspects of the industry are sophisticated, including structuring for tax efficiency and legal issues, but for the most part, once you have done it the first time (i.e., set up a hedge fund), it is like riding a bike: You never forget how it works and what needs to be done.

Although investors may initially assume that hedge funds and mutual funds operate in a similar fashion, in reality the only similarity between the funds is that both operate as pooled investment vehicles. This means that a number of investors entrust their money to a manager for a specific fund that goes out and buys and sells securities in order to make a profit.

Hedge funds differ from mutual funds in that investors provide hedge fund managers with the ability to pursue absolute return strategies. Mutual funds generally offer only relative return strategies.

An *absolute return strategy* is the new name for the strategy that Jones invented in the late 1940s. It means that regardless of market conditions, a hedge fund manager will make money. This differs from what is called a *relative return strategy*, which is how one fund does against a benchmark. In recent years there have been a number of indices created to track and benchmark hedge funds. While these products are good, they are not flawless. Therefore, it is best to think of hedge funds as vehicles that are measured on their specific performance, not on how their performance is relative to the S&P 500 Index or the Lipper Small Cap Index or any other benchmark used to measure performance of traditional investments.

Mutual funds, due to their structure and the laws that govern how they operate, invest in a predefined style and strategies such as large-cap growth and mid-cap value or a particular sector such as the utilities or biotechnology. The mutual fund defines its strategy and style in its prospectus, which is given to existing and prospective investors. Manager performance is measured on how a fund's return compares to that of a specific index or benchmark. For example, if you buy into a large-cap value fund, the managers of that fund try to outperform the S&P 500 Index.

Most mutual fund managers construct portfolios by using their stock-picking skills to create a portfolio that they believe will perform well over time and in turn provide them with an edge over the index. All they need to do is to outperform the index by a few basis points and they are deemed to be good at what they do. That being said, mutual fund managers have one goal in mind when they manage their money: beating their relative index. If the index is down 10 percent while the mutual fund is down only 7 percent, the fund's performance would be called a success. The press would anoint these managers as heroes of the money management industry and they would be deemed to be "expert" stock pickers because they beat their relative benchmark. The problem is, as an investor, you can't eat relative returns. In the preceding scenario, you would have lost 7 percent of your investment, plus fees, to these heroes' "expert ability" to pick stocks!

Hedge funds are completely opposite. Hedge funds are managed to seek positive absolute returns, regardless of the performance of an index or sector benchmark. Unlike mutual funds, which are long only (meaning they are able to make only a buy or sell decision), a hedge fund is able to implement more aggressive strategies and put on positions that include short selling. Managers may also employ derivatives instruments, such as options, and use leverage to enhance the portfolio and add to the positive performance of the bottom line.

Due to their ability to short, many believe that hedge funds are more popular in bear markets than in bull markets. However, in 2005 this was not the case. For the most part, hedge funds performed quite poorly for the 11 months ending November 30, 2005, and eked out only single-digit positive numbers for the month of December. This meant that numbers for the year were not good. Some funds were unable to take advantage of the volatility that markets experienced in the wake of the increase in oil and other commodity prices and the geopolitical uncertainty that stemmed from U.S. military operations in Afghanistan and Iraq. Consequently, 2005 proved to be a very difficult year for hedge funds. The year was disappointing for almost everyone who invested in these products. Many fund managers looked forward to 2006 and to the idea of being able to fight another day. However, in the wake of the continued volatility that the markets experienced in the first six months of 2006, managers and investors were disappointed with the performance results of most funds. Most investors believe that because hedge funds have the ability to go long and short and really use any tool necessary to achieve their returns, they should do well regardless of whether the market is bullish or bearish.

Performance measurement is not the only difference between the two investment vehicles. Mutual funds are either open-ended investment companies that sell their shares to the masses through multiple marketing channels or are closed end, which trade on an exchange. Hedge funds do not operate this way. Hedge funds are limited to the number of investors they can have, either 100 or 500, depending on their structure, and are open only to accredited investors or qualified purchasers. For the most part, hedge funds in the United States are either limited partnerships or limited liability companies that are investment vehicles exempt from the Securities Act of 1933, herein referred to as the Thirty-three Act. Later chapters will discuss specific structures and domiciles. For now, just think of all hedge funds as limited liability companies, or LLCs.

Hedge fund investors need to understand that these investment vehicles have significantly different fee structures and liquidity provisions than mutual funds. The liquidity provisions vary, but for the most part it is difficult for an investor to redeem his or her investment at will. Most funds operate on quarterly redemptions and usually enforce a one-year lockup. If violated, this carries a hefty penalty or redemption fee—usually 1 percent of assets. Unlike mutual funds, hedge funds are not registered under the Thirty-three Act, and thus they are prohibited from soliciting or advertising to the general public. This prohibition tends to reinforce the popular press's notion that the hedge fund industry is secretive or mysterious. The press also likes to call into question the fees associated with hedge fund investing, labeling these investment vehicles as "expensive." Unlike mutual funds, which are governed by the Investment Company Act of 1940 according to explicit rules about fees and how they are charged, hedge funds are not subject to these restrictions and regulations.

For the most part, hedge funds typically charge a management fee equal to 1 or 1.5 percent of assets under management, along with an incentive fee—usually 20 percent—of the profits of the portfolio. As a side note, Jones did not charge a management fee; he charged only an incentive, or a profit-participation, fee. A number of hedge fund managers implemented the management fee in the late 1960s as a way to ensure business continuity.

Copies of both the Thirty-three Act and the Forty Act can be found online by simply Googling the information. You should read and become familiar with both of these documents as you build your business. The Forty Act governs the way all money management vehicles are marketed, sold, and operated in the United States. It stipulates who can and cannot buy certain products and how those products need to be administered and operated by the individuals or corporations who own, sell, and market them. In certain cases, including right now, for example, it should be made clear that some money management firms market registered hedge funds that are similar in structure to mutual funds and are available for the masses. However, for the purposes of this book, I will not be talking about such products. I focus solely on funds that are not registered and, as such, are exempt from the Thirty-three Act. Two specific characteristics provide for this exemption:

1. The number of investors that may be accepted into the fund
2. The type of investor that is acceptable

All funds are limited to either 100 or 500 investors and are open to either accredited or superaccredited investors, also known as *qualified purchasers*. As of early 2006, the definitions of an accredited investor and a superaccredited or qualified purchaser are as follows. An *accredited investor* must be one of the following: (1) a financial institution, (2) an affiliate of the issuer, or (3) an individual with a net worth of at least $1 million or an annual income of at least $200,000, and the investment must not account for more than 20 percent of the investor's worth.[6] A *qualified purchaser* is any of the following: (1) a natural person who owns $5 million or more in net investments, (2) any person, acting for his or her own account or for the accounts of other qualified purchasers who, in the aggregate, own and invest on a discretionary basis not less than $25,000,000 in net investments, (3) any family-owned organization or entity that owns $5 million or more in net investments, and (4) any trust that was not formed for the specific purpose of acquiring the securities offered, as to which each trustee and person who contributed assets to the trust meets the previous requirements.[7] However, as of the summer of 2006, in the wake of the Goldstein decision (which I discuss in detail later in this chapter), the SEC was considering changing the rules that define accredited investors and was in the process of proposing new definitions for these investors.

The definition has remained the same for quite some time. However, there has been some talk among industry observers that once the hedge fund registration requirement put in place in February 2006 is fully digested, the SEC will look at changing the definition of an accredited investor to further limit who can invest in hedge funds.

While these rules define who can and cannot invest in hedge funds, it needs to be made clear that managers have the ability to accept nonaccredited investors into their funds as long as they limit their number to fewer than 35 individuals.

SEC Regulation D stipulates that a maximum of 35 nonaccredited investors are allowed to invest money into a private placement (i.e., a hedge fund). However, most managers do not allow for nonaccredited investors, because in doing so they are giving away investment slots that could go to other, more-well-heeled investors who could provide more money to manage.

One hedge fund accountant who tracks the industry said that having nonaccredited investors in the fund could become a regulatory issue, but it is also a bad business decision because of the limited amount of money they can give a manager to manage.

"Managers are better off sticking with people who meet the investment requirement and who can afford to give them significant chunks of money to invest so that they can build their business," he said. "If they let all 35 nonaccredited investors in the fund, they are really limiting their ability to grow their business."

Hedge funds have operated in relative obscurity for the better part of the past 50 years because they are not registered investment vehicles and because they are open only to accredited and superaccredited investors. However, to understand how hedge funds have come into the mainstream, we need to look at how Wall Street has evolved since the stock market crash of 1987.

HEDGE FUND HISTORY

Over the past 50 years, the hedge fund industry has grown at a significant but quiet pace. The industry grew steadily from the 1950s to the mid-1970s and then hit a plateau of sorts for most of the 1980s. However, in the post-crash euphoria and as Wall Street kissed the 1980s goodbye, traders, brokers, and bankers began to realize that the go-go days were truly over. They looked for an alternative to their traditional income streams, and what they found was the hedge fund industry.

In late 1987 and for most of 1988, there was not much of a hedge fund industry. However, a number of very smart and forward-thinking Wall Streeters saw the writing on the wall. This group of brokers, lawyers, and accountants collectively decided to begin pushing something called *prime brokerage*. Prime brokerage, which will be discussed in detail in Chapter 2, is a service that basically allows the trader to trade and the money manager to manage money, leaving pretty much all back-office functions of running a fund to a third party. Large, well-respected Wall Street brokerage firms had been providing prime brokerage services for years, which accounted for a small but significant part of their bottom line. Next to clearing, prime brokerage is one of the most profitable services that firms can offer. Not only is it quite profitable, it is also nearly risk free, making its profits that much more attractive. For years, only the big firms offered their services to hedge funds. However, in the wake of the crash, a number of smaller, more aggressive firms decided that what they needed to do was to provide prime brokerage services not only to large, well-respected firms that were already running successful hedge funds, but also to basically anyone who wanted to be in the hedge fund business.

"There was a consensus that prime brokerage could provide a steady stream of, for the most part, riskless income to the firm," said one former prime brokerage executive. "So what we decided to do was to get the word out that starting a hedge fund was easy, not too expensive, and that we could help anyone who wanted to get into the business."

One interesting fact about the hedge fund business is that it is the great equalizer. Literally anyone can get into it as long as they have the money to pay the lawyers and can get some investors who are willing to entrust them with their assets. That is why the industry has been and will remain so attractive to people from all walks of Wall Street and beyond. It is truly the only business that allows anyone to literally hang out a shingle regardless of experience or education. That being said, every time there is a prolonged bear market, the hedge fund industry explodes. It is truly easy to get into the game that is now the hedge fund industry. The question is, can you stay there? While later chapters discuss at length how to survive, remember that the name of the game is assets. If you cannot raise assets and attract investors, then you are destined for death. But if you can build a track record, attract investor interest, and in turn draw in their assets, you are destined for hedge fund greatness—and with this greatness comes vast riches. That is why in the wake of the crash of 1987 there was movement by brokerage firms to push prime brokerage services and get people excited about the opportunities that existed in running, owning, and investing in a hedge fund.

To understand what happened in the hedge fund industry, think of the phenomenon that is Texas Hold'em and how it has taken hold of the card-playing public around the world.

It is believed that poker was imported to the United States by French fur traders and explorers in the nineteenth century. While no one seems to know for sure, it is expected that the origins of the game come from the Persian game As Nas.[8] According to some poker historians, the first known direct reference to poker was made in New Orleans in the 1830s. It spread from there up and down the Mississippi and Ohio rivers and became a thing of lore among cowboys on the Western frontier.

While people had been playing poker and various types of the games for years, Texas Hold'em became popular among gamblers and card players in the early 1970s with the World Series of Poker at Binions Casino in Las Vegas. Over the years, the tournament grew and established itself around the world as the premier tournament for poker players. The game and the tournament continued to grow in popularity throughout the 1980s and 1990s, but exploded in the early part of the twenty-first century. This was due to the confluence of a number of events, primarily television, the Internet, and some forward-thinking casino executives. For years, the tournament had been televised by a number of local outlets and on ESPN, but in 2003 it made its debut on the Travel Channel and picked up a huge following.[9] Like hedge funds, Texas Hold'em has a low barrier to entry. It is literally open to anyone who has the money to get into the game. Furthermore, Texas Hold'em offers great riches to those who are successful at it. The turning point for Texas Hold'em came in 2003, when the winner of the World Series of Poker was Chris Moneymaker, a relative novice in the game who gained his entry to the tournament through his successful play on the Internet. The idea that a person playing the game on a computer could sit down with the best live players in the world and beat them set the game on a path to the moon. Sound familiar? Think novice hedge fund managers who pick great stocks! Today Texas Hold'em is fast becoming the most popular casino game in gambling dens around the country and has become a mainstay on mainstream television stations like Fox, NBC, and ESPN, which broadcast tournaments year-round.[10]

The parallels between the growth in the hedge fund industry and the growth in Texas Hold'em are significant. Just as a few computer programmers, television executives, and casino operators decided to push an old game to a new audience in an effort to bring a new level of excitement to online and in-person gambling, a number of brokerage firms, lawyers, and accountants decided to make it very easy to get into the hedge fund business and pushed the barrier of entry low enough to make it worth the financial risk associated with the transaction. But unlike those who pushed Texas Hold'em through the Internet and tournament play, those who pushed the hedge fund industry did it through seminars and cocktail parties. In the early 1990s, it was next to impossible to find a Monday, Tuesday, or Wednesday afternoon in which a brokerage firm, along with lawyers and accountants, was not offering a seminar and cocktail hour on how to get into the hedge fund business.

Going into the late 1980s and early 1990s, the hedge fund industry grew from being a relative afterthought for many to something that was front and center to most people on the Street. The growth was spurred by the uncertainty of the markets, the lack of perceived riches from the Wall

Street firms, and a lack of good jobs for many. The large firms significantly scaled back their operations in light of the crash and let lots of people go. In addition, they scaled back compensation to those who remained employed. More people were out of work, which meant that more people became entrepreneurs. This, coupled with an explosion of lawyers, accountants, and prime brokers who saw an opportunity in offering services to hedge funds, combined to make the perfect storm that led to the industry's explosive growth. The excitement surrounding the opportunity in the hedge fund industry was a direct result of the service providers' realization that there was, and still is, very little risk that cannot be quantified when you are working with a hedge fund. This means that while they could lose clients because individual funds did not perform and in turn were unable to raise assets, it would be very hard for them to lose their broader business as long as a constant flow of new managers cropped up. Therefore, service providers needed to get the word out and make it easy for managers to get up and running. The brokers quickly realized that one hedge fund manager who blew up could not take down an entire firm like a rogue trader using firm capital could. They determined that the business risk was and is limited to a hit to the bottom line in terms of fee income, but that a blowup cannot truly destroy the business. In the worst-case scenario, the lawyer, accountant, prime broker, and administrator would simply need to find new clients to replace the lost income that the dead funds had provided.

Throughout the 1990s and into the new millennium, many service providers came to realize that they needed to be able to meet the needs of managers, not only to continue to survive on Wall Street, but also to take advantage of the significant fee income that is generated by these financial vehicles that are often thought of as mysterious and secretive. The barrier to entry is so low that there has been an explosion in the number of people getting into the business—it costs around $50,000[11] or so to create and launch a fund, which means almost anyone can do it. Along with the low cost to enter come huge financial rewards for the manager and his or her team if they can build a successful business. There are few areas of employment in which people can earn so much so fast for their efforts. The press makes us gasp every time a professional athlete signs a huge contract, but in truth, while their salaries and bonuses are undoubtedly large, this money pales in comparison to what a hedge fund manager and his or her traders can earn in a single year. Some of the most respected and envied people on Wall Street—or any street, for that matter—are hedge fund managers who earn hundreds of millions of dollars for their work in the markets in a single year. As the number of funds increases, so does the number of service providers offering tools to help the managers be successful. And it becomes a numbers game. Fees contract while the number of clients expands—

meaning they need more and more people to provide services to hedge funds, which means the industry keeps growing and growing. Eventually something will come along that will cause the pace of fund growth to slow. But for now, until the fees generated by the industry subside, lots of people will be pushing other people to get into the hedge fund business.

It is clear that unlimited riches await the budding yet successful manager. And therein lies the main issue: Not everyone can or will be successful. There are two reasons for this. First, not everyone can really trade or invest successfully. Simply put, some hedge fund managers cannot earn the returns that investors have come to expect. Second, some managers are simply unable to raise enough money to keep their businesses afloat because they are unable to perform. The hardest part of being in the hedge fund business is raising capital. Very few people can do it successfully. Many people say they can raise money and promise to be able to help a fund get started, but most of them fail to deliver. Marketing and raising capital are explored later in the book. It is Chapter 6 that should not be missed because it is the most important part of running a successful business.

WHAT'S NEW

In October 2004, for one of the first times in the history of the Securities and Exchange Commission, the commissioners split their votes, three to two, along party lines to change the regulation and require all hedge fund managers who meet specific requirements to register as *registered investment advisers* (RIAs). The vote was historic in that it is rare for the commissioners not to vote unanimously on rule changes.

The vote, thought of as controversial by some, required hedge fund advisers to register as investment advisers by February 2006. In the wake of the ruling, a number of industry insiders and trade groups sought to challenge its legitimacy. One hedge fund manager challenged the ruling in court. In December 2005, a U.S. Court of Appeals for the District of Columbia heard arguments against the ruling. Its decision to strike down the SEC registration rule came down on June 23, 2006, vacating the rule and sending it back to the commission to reconsider its regulation. The action was brought by Phillip Goldstein, manager of the hedge fund Opportunity Partners LP. He argued that the SEC did not have authority to adopt the rule and that it misinterpreted a previous portion of the law that had exempted hedge funds from registration. The news of the decision by the D.C. Court of Appeals sent shock waves across both sides of the registration aisle. Both camps—those for the registration rule and those against it—seemed to be in disbelief that it had been struck down.

The *Wall Street Journal* summed it best by calling Goldstein's efforts "a David versus Goliath fight: "He took on the Commission on his own, no other managers joined him in the suit and he paid for it out of his own pocket—an expense of nearly $300,000."[12]

Prior to the court's ruling, many managers believed that the SEC would not stop with the regulation, but would ultimately require hedge funds themselves, and not just their advisers, to register with the SEC, similar to the way that a mutual fund is registered. Another smaller but still important concern is that the perceived additional administrative costs created by registration would raise the barrier to entry in the industry, stifling entrepreneurship. The latter was an objection raised by then–Federal Reserve chairman Alan Greenspan in early 2004 when the SEC was accepting comments on the rule change and he was asked about the pending registration issue.

At the time, the SEC commissioners acknowledged the potential issue with entrepreneurship by exempting advisers of hedge funds with fewer than 15 clients or less than $25 million in assets from registering. This was their equitable solution to the little guy.

However, since the ruling, the hedge fund industry seems to believe that it no longer has to deal with the registration issue. Although some believed that the SEC would try to circumvent the court ruling, possibly turning to Congress or the states for relief or guidance on how to create and implement a registration requirement, by the midsummer of 2006, it looked like this effort would go nowhere.

From February 2006, when the rule went into effect, until late June, the industry had been operating under the assumption that the regulation was fixed in place. Managers who had not already registered as investment advisers went through the process in order to stay in the business. As registered investment advisers, these hedge fund managers had to adopt basic compliance controls, improve their disclosures to investors, and open their doors to the SEC for periodic audits—no different than what is required of mutual fund managers. The regulation would also allow the SEC to be able to collect and make public basic information, including the assets and identities of U.S.-based hedge fund managers.

In the wake of the ruling, the debate goes on. Some observers believe that the registration requirement needs to be resurrected, that it does not go far enough, and that it does not address marketing issues that have caused some investors to stay away from hedge funds. Other investors believe that the regulation is a move in the right direction, but that because hedge funds are illiquid, have a management- and incentive-fee structure, and do not provide transparency, the registration does little if anything to increase their interest in these investment vehicles. Many industry observers believe, however, that these types of rules will not deter fraud because the SEC and its staff are overextended and cannot complete the work that they already have. The SEC's response to this is that it will hire and put in place the resources needed to monitor and enforce the regulation. However, a study by the Government Accountability Office found that the SEC was able to review just 23 percent of all corporate fillings in 2003.[13] In 2002, Congress passed a law requiring the SEC to review all public companies at least once every three years. Therefore, critics of the new regulation question how the SEC will be able to deal with the added burden of monitoring thousands of hedge fund managers. However, when the SEC made the ruling, it was estimated that nearly 40 percent of hedge fund advisers were already registered with the SEC. Funds that had preregistered with the SEC were institutions that targeted pension, endowment, and foundation money.

The reason for this is that managers believe the assets that these institutions put to work are some of the best that are out there. Often, these types of institutions make sizable allocations, and their assets are usually quite sticky. It is money that is very lucrative and very difficult to come by but also easy to keep. Once these institutions make an allocation to a fund, they very rarely move the money. These types of investors use consultants who, for the most part, operate within a check-the-box mentality. This means that in order for a fund to qualify for the beauty contest that takes place prior to the allocation, it needs to meet all of the requirements the consultants and their clients have deemed necessary for their money. One of those requirements has been that the manager be an RIA. The reason for this is that the marketplace puts a high degree of significance on funds that are run by RIAs, who are perceived to be more professional than those who are not RIAs.

The perception is quite different from the reality. The reality is that almost anyone who meets certain requirements can—and, in most cases, is forced to—register. The registration process consists of filling out and filing a Form ADV and complying with the rules set forth by the SEC governing registered investment advisers. In the past, hedge fund managers generally registered with the SEC when they had $25 million or more in client assets. In some cases, an adviser with less than $25 million was forced to register with state securities regulators based on the location of the principal place of business. This aspect of the registration requirement varies from state to state. Nevertheless, if a manager wanted money from an endowment, pension, or foundation, he or she needed to be registered, and, because of the power of these assets, the manager registered willingly.

The funds that led the challenge to the registration requirement were organizations that believed the ruling would put undue pressure on them. With the adoption of the rule, hedge fund managers needed to comply with and operate under strict guidelines that truly dictate how they operate their businesses. This means additional costs in both human and nonhuman capital. For example, businesses now have to put in place a compliance manual that details how the organization is run in the front, middle, and back offices. They have to install a chief compliance officer whose job it is to ensure that the fund and its employees are operating appropriately in regard to accepting assets, putting assets to work, and tracking all communication between investors, potential investors, and their surrogates. In some cases, the regulation on the professional side of the organization will help the funds operate more efficiently, while other aspects of the regulation are a real hindrance and could be a significant financial burden to the firm's operation.

The complaints notwithstanding, some believe that the regulation will actually help the industry and bring it more into the mainstream. However, the registration requirement is also expected to put investors more at ease with investing in hedge funds. In my opinion, this provides a false sense of security to investors with little or no experience with this type of product. Some believe that just because a fund manager is registered, the investment is worthwhile. This is similar to saying that just because you have a driver's license you are qualified to drive in the Indianapolis 500. We all know that this is just not the case in either scenario. Registration is not a seal of approval. It simply means that the manager filled out some paperwork, completed a compliance review, and is willing to be audited randomly by the SEC. It does not mean the fund is worthy of investor assets. Unfortunately, as funds become more and more mainstream and as they start to look more and more alike, investors are going to have to do stronger and more thorough due diligence. The question is, can and will they be willing to do it?

As a manager, your job is to run your business in the most efficient and cost-effective manner possible. Your job is to evaluate the costs associated with registering versus the fees that could be generated on assets raised because your fund now was able to check the box. However, that will no longer be the case, and with the new rules comes a level playing field of sorts for managers of all strategies and sizes.

Hedge funds have caught the eye of regulators because of the explosive growth the industry experienced in the new millennium. The SEC estimated that there were nearly 8,500 funds operating in 2005, with more than $1 trillion in assets under management.[14] This clearly means the industry is no longer just a private club for wealthy investors and their friends, as it was in the first 30 years of the product's life. Now hedge funds are mainstream and part of almost every investor's vernacular. Hedge funds both large and small have filled the role vacated by the large brokerage firms that shut down their propriety trading desks, and they now provide liquidity and capital to the marketplace. Today, hedge fund managers are the people making markets and allowing the markets to move forward; they are the money managers who are looking for global opportunities to exploit while simultaneously providing liquidity.

With or without registration or regulation, the hedge fund industry is here to stay. Hedge fund managers and their investors will be around in one way, shape, or form for the rest of our lives. The question is, how will the industry evolve as markets change and investor appetites become more and more refined? With this in mind, there are a number of issues that you, as a budding manager, need to address before you decide to go out on your own.

First, you need to have what it takes to be an entrepreneur. Second, you need to make sure you have the financial backing to build and maintain a sustainable business and to ensure that you can actually deliver on the promises that you are making to investors in your offering documents. Third, you need to hire a genuinely qualified team of service providers to help you realize your dream.

MAKING IT ON YOUR OWN

Whether you have the skills to be an entrepreneur is difficult to know. Being an entrepreneur is even harder when you have previously worked for a large company and have been long exposed to the corporate world. Some hedge fund managers don't like the fact that in their new company they will have to be the chief cook *and* the bottle washer. These managers just want to be able to pick up the phone and get results from a network. Ultimately, such people don't make it in the hedge fund world. In order to make it, you need to be willing to roll up your sleeves and get involved in all aspects of your business and its operation. Taking an active role in all aspects of your business will make you more likely to succeed.

Nancy Havens, of Havens Partners, a $500 million fund in New York, told me while I was interviewing her for a profile in one of my other books, *Getting Started in Hedge Funds*, that the hardest thing about going out on her own was realizing that she did not matter to anyone anymore. She could not simply pick up the phone and get her computer fixed or a new cartridge for the printer. As an entrepreneur heading her own company, she was no longer part of the machine that is Bear Stearns. She now does the day-to-day tasks herself.

"It was hard to get used to this," she said. "But after a while, I got a better understanding of how important infrastructure is and how to get things done on this side of the business."[15]

DELIVERING ON YOUR PROMISE TO INVESTORS

When you start a hedge fund, you need to be able to seed the fund with some assets—yours, your friends', and your family's—and you need working capital to ensure that you stay in business. Raising money (as you will find out soon enough if you do not already know) is probably the hardest part of any business. Remember, those you think will give you money most likely will not, and people whom you never in a million years believed would step up to plate will do so. In most entrepreneurs' experience, that is just the way it works. In order to get investors and, more important, keep them, you need to first have a good, solid strategy that is clearly defined in your offering documents and marketing materials. Then you need to deliver on it. If you can't execute your strategy, don't start the fund. It does not matter if you are successful (i.e., put up positive numbers); it is more important that you do what you say you are going to do. Investors are willing to forgive you and stick with you if you make mistakes or the strategy does not work. But once you drift away from the stated strategy, you might as well look for a new job working for someone else. Investors have little or no tolerance for this kind of behavior.

"The markets don't allow managers to always be successful," says Richard Bookbinder, the manager of a New York–based fund of funds. "The idea is to find a strategy that can work over time and a manager who does not stray from it simply in hopes of putting up better numbers. I would much rather have a manager tell me that the strategy did not work because of this, this, and this, than have him or her tell me that they tried a new strategy midmonth and made a lot of money. I want to know that what I invest in is what I am getting."

Strategies and styles aside, one thing both individual and institutional investors alike are looking at during the due diligence process is the service providers the fund uses to conduct its business.

You want to see that both new and old funds use good, solid, and well-respected service provider partners as their lawyers, prime brokers, auditors, and administrators. The main reason investors like to see who the fund is doing business with is that there have been a number of cases of fraud at firms such as Bayou, KL, and Beacon Hill over the past few years. Subsequently, there is a common belief that if respected firms are providing audit, administration, legal, and prime brokerage services to funds, they must have passed some level of due diligence. Unfortunately, the reality is that you never know, and therefore you should not take anything a manager says at face value.

About a year ago, I was at a hedge fund conference in Boca Raton, Florida, and during the four-day hedge fund lovefest, I was approached by the manager of a fund of funds who was looking for a strategic partnership with a large institution. The manager had gotten my name from a mutual friend, who told him about a number of projects that my firm had worked on that were similar to his. Similarly, he needed to take his business to the next level and thought it made sense for us to meet.

My friend, the manager, and I decided to go to lunch to see if there was something we could do together. During the meal, we talked about a number of things regarding the industry: how he perceived the partnership would work, what he wanted out of the deal, and who he had already talked with about partnering. All in all, the conversation went very smoothly, and the lunch looked like it would turn out to be a profitable one for both of us.

The next step for me was to get a copy of the funds' documents, review their performance, and think about ideas on how to help the manager with his problem. A significant part of this research was to do some crude but significant due diligence on the manager, his fund, and the organization. The initial work would be based on a review of and contact with his lawyer and administrator.

A few days after we had lunch, the documents arrived in my office, and I immediately scanned the name of the fund's service providers. As it turns out, the fund's lawyer was my firm's fund counsel—small world. As an aside, for the most part, all fund documents are the same, so it is very easy to review a document rather quickly. A hedge fund document starts with a number of disclaimers, then moves into the summary of the offering, followed by a detailed explanation of the summary. The summary of the offering always states the fund's auditor, administrator, lawyer, prime broker, and any other service providers of substance who may be working with or for the fund in its ongoing operation. (A thorough list of service providers can be found on the Internet. You can also e-mail me at das@hedgean swers.com for some names that may help you get started.)

After reading the document, reviewing the marketing material, and talking to my partner about the opportunity, I called our lawyer to find out what he knew about this fund he counseled. The lawyer said, "I know the fund and the manager. We wrote the documents about six or seven years ago, but I have not heard from him since. Is he still in business?"

He also told me that now that he had heard his name was still in the document, he was going to call the manager to catch up and see how they could restore the relationship. This type of situation is quite normal. It is not a red flag but rather a fact of life; once a document is completed, there is little, if any, work that the fund and the lawyers do together unless there is a problem or the business is expanding.

Maybe this manager had no questions and, more important, no problems during their lack of contact, or maybe he found a different lawyer to work with and did not want the new lawyer to rewrite the documents. It was something my partner and I would question in one of our follow-up conversations.

During this particular due diligence we found nothing that led us to believe that anything was wrong with the relationship. The fund and the lawyer had simply gone their separate ways. The manager had been minding his business, making investments, and gathering assets and had no need for this particular law firm or its counsel.

The point of this story is that as a person who is looking to build a successful business, you need to be prepared and have answers for investors who pick up the phone and make inquiries to you about your firm. You need to make sure that you have all the answers to the questions before you are asked them, and, furthermore, you should make sure that you never misrepresent anything to prospective investors. It is important that you are on top of your relationships with service providers and that they are aware that you are using them for references. You don't ever want to be caught in a situation where the information offered by the service provider is different from the information that you give to your investor, or one in which the service provider does not know how your two firms are working together. The key is to be prepared for all scenarios.

Unfortunately or fortunately, the service provider industry has grown quite substantially over the past five years. It seems everyone is getting into the business of providing products and services to hedge funds. Chapter 2 covers the role of the service provider and how you, as a start-up manager, should select and work with various service providers as you build your organization.

CHAPTER 2

The Service Providers

T oday in the United States, most hedge funds have four different groups of service providers. Each fund manager has a lawyer, a prime broker, an audit firm, and usually an administrator. In some cases, hedge funds also hire outside marketers, compliance consultants, and technology specialists.

By name, each of the providers listed here is recognizable and probably needs no further explanation. However, in today's environment—with registration in place and more and more regulation coming down the pike—it is important for you to realize the role each plays in a successful organization. As a manager, you need to have top-notch firms that will provide good, solid, and exceptional service to your fund, regardless of market conditions. And you need to make sure you work with name-brand organizations. In today's competitive environment, many investors do business only with funds using service providers they have experience with from past investments.

This chapter explores the role of each of the preceding groups of service providers. The idea is to give you a basic but thorough understanding of the function each will play in your organization and how you can use them to your advantage as you grow and expand your business. In the final section of this chapter, I discuss a fifth group of service providers— the marketers—exploring the role that outside or third-party marketers can play in building your business and presenting the pros and cons of using them in your organization.

TYPES OF PROVIDERS

Once you decide to get into the hedge fund business, you will need to first put together a business plan that outlines how the fund is going to be structured, how you are going to manage the assets, and how you are going to raise the assets. The first stop on the path to the hedge fund business that most people make is to a prime broker.

21

The prime broker usually serves as a good starting point for people who are new to going it alone and need help to get things going. The prime broker, along with providing you with execution services, will also be a resource for information to contact and establish relationships with other service providers. Initially, finding a prime broker may be very difficult. Many large firms will say that they do not want to work with start-ups; many smaller firms are start-ups themselves and have little or no track record to enable you to determine whether they will be able to provide the service and executions that your fund will need to launch and be successful. The choice is a difficult one that will require serious consideration as you continue down the path to fund launch.

Because of weak hedge fund performance in 2005 and new registration requirements, the number of new fund start-ups in early 2006 seemed to be decreasing or at least leveling off. As a result, a number of prime brokers were seeing their new business decline. Prior to this time, the number of firms offering prime brokerage services had exploded, meaning that as a new hedge fund manager, you were entering a buyer's market!

The lawyer is usually the second stop on your path to hedge fund greatness. However, it is the first service provider discussed in detail in this chapter, because the lawyer is the person you will spend the most time with in the early days of your business. The lawyer will provide you with a blueprint for what will eventually become your fund and your management company.

Over the past few years, lawyers have changed the structure of choice for funds from a limited partnership (LP) to a limited liability company (LLC). Either structure will work and is acceptable. However, currently many lawyers believe that an LLC offers a higher level of protection from investors in the event that something goes wrong and there is litigation.

The accountant is your third stop on your path to building a hedge fund. An accountant will provide you with insight and guidance on how fees are calculated and paid, how you deal with taxes, and how to audit your performance.

The administrator is generally the last service provider you will talk to as you make your way to launching your fund. The administrator will keep your books and records, help you keep track of investors, and prepare your performance reports on a monthly and quarterly basis.

The final service provider you might meet with is a marketer. I am not a big believer in marketers. I have met very few over the years who can actually deliver in assets. However, some are very good, and the those are the ones who can raise money for your fund and help you attract investors.

LAWYERS

The lawyer's job is to guide you and your business partners through the process of drafting the offering and business documents of the fund and setting up the organization that will become the money management firm. The documents include, but are not limited to, an offering memorandum (this is the first document you draft), a subscription document, and a limited liability company agreement.

The *offering memorandum* describes the fund, how it trades, how it operates, and all of the details of the organization. This document is similar to a mutual fund prospectus. The *subscription document* is what investors fill out to invest in the fund. Although it does include information on the fund, it requires potential investors to answer many questions about who they are, their objectives, and their investing knowledge. The *limited liability company agreement* details how the company (i.e., the fund) is run, who is responsible for what functions, and the role of the investor in the company.

Each document serves a specific function in the operation and management of the company and details the relationship between the fund, its manager, and its investors. Examples of the documents can be found on the Web at www.hedgeanswers.com. The documents are quite long and detailed and at first glance seem both boring and repetitive. The documents detail investment strategy, provide descriptions of the management team, and examine risks involved with the investment.

Without a doubt, the lawyer will include everything that could go wrong—and then some—in this section of the document. Other areas to pay attention to during the review process are the way in which fees are calculated and paid to the management company, how the fund's style and strategy are described, and tax issues and considerations. The accountant will help you with the fee and tax areas. You and your partners will be the only ones who can determine whether the style and strategy sections are correct.

It is very important to have a full understanding of all aspects of the documents. Each contains specific issues governing the business and its operation. You need to be familiar with the material so you can fulfill your fiduciary responsibilities to your investors and so you can communicate to potential investors clearly, concisely, and accurately.

As the hedge fund industry has grown over the past few years, the documents have often become boilerplate. Very little new insight is now being written into offering memorandums or subscription agreements. That is a direct result of the fact that very little has changed in partnership law and taxation regulations over the past five or six years. As new laws are passed and regulations come into force, the lawyers update the documents to reflect these changes.

Most new managers think that they are getting something unique from their lawyers when in reality all they are getting is a document that is updated with their pertinent information. While some might not like this, it is good from a litigation standpoint. Should something go wrong, it is better for the manager to have a document that is similar to other offerings than something so unique that it stands out within the industry. This is also true from a marketing standpoint. Sophisticated investors know what to look for in the document and this gives them great comfort. If it is not like what they have seen before, it might take longer for them to review it and make a decision to invest.

Today a hedge fund can have its documents completed for as little as $15,000 to $25,000, or a new manager can spend close to $100,000.[1] It all depends on the law firm that is chosen to write the documents and the amount of legal work required to complete the process. Some lawyers will say—off the record, of course—that less expensive firms provide flawed documents and that pricier documents are flawless and as close to perfect as possible. As someone who has worked with both the expensive and the less expensive lawyers, my comment is as follows: Work with the lawyer with whom you feel most comfortable and to whom you think you will matter most. In the end, paying a lot of money does not mean that you are getting a better product than what you would get if you bought a less expensive one; it just means it will cost more. I believe that because the hedge fund industry has gotten so big so fast, there is very little difference in the type of product you will get from the law firms that offer hedge fund services. Therefore, base your decision on what fits best with your needs, whom you feel most comfortable talking to about your business, and who you think will give you the best advice going forward.

Initially, you will spend an enormous amount of time working with lawyers on documents that will develop your idea into a viable hedge fund. The work will entail going over the strategy, the style, how it works, and what instruments will be used to achieve the fund's performance goals. You will also need to work on things like your biography and those of your partners. It is important that you like the lawyers, respect them, and believe in their ability to get the job done. If the relationship is acrimonious, the process will take too long and will not yield the product you need to be successful.

You want a lawyer who provides insight and good answers to your questions. You want someone who is a reliable resource when you have a question about something in the business that may be legal in nature, although unrelated to the document, and you want someone who can guide you smoothly through the process.

"The first lawyer we met with really seemed to not want to work with us," said one manager, who asked for anonymity. "He gave us a quote that we thought was completely unreasonable, and when we asked him why it was so high, he said, 'That is the price, take it or leave it.' We left it. We went with another firm that we had heard good things about and who was willing to work with us in a manner that made us feel extremely comfortable."

This particular manager met with three lawyers before deciding which firm met his needs. Choosing service providers can be a very nerve-racking and annoying process. However, the first rule in choosing a service provider is to remember that you are the customer and that the customer is always right.

Service providers need you just as much as you need them. No one knows how successful or unsuccessful a new fund is going to be and, subsequently, how big a client your impending fund may become. Don't do business with those who do not believe in you and what you are about to do. They will not make good service providers.

The best way to choose a lawyer is to meet with a number of them and get a feel for them. One lawyer I met with when I was starting a fund of funds was someone I had known for many years. He had a decent reputation and was someone I thought was very strong in this area. When I sat down with him to discuss the project, he seemed very interested, listened intently, but also took a number of phone calls and typed out messages on his BlackBerry. The meeting—which probably needed to be no longer than 40 minutes—lasted well over an hour because we were interrupted so many times. Finally after about 45 minutes of nonsense, I asked him if he wanted me to come back later because he was so busy and he replied, "No, this is how it always is." When my partner and I left, we looked at each other and said, "This guy is not for us." He is probably a great lawyer. He is a friend in the business. But he is also someone who did not make us feel comfortable as potential clients. The lawyer we chose for this specific project turned out to be a good, solid, though expensive, choice. His work was exceptional, but it was mostly done by associates, one of whom left us in the middle of the project, which made things more difficult. However, in the end, we were very happy with the result. Our only regret was that the associate had not stayed through to the end; we appreciated the quality of her work.

What do lawyers do for all the money you pay them? They are going to create and put in place the structure that will become your business. The lawyer will establish the company and provide you with corporate documents to establish the infrastructure of your business. In some cases, the lawyer will also secure your tax ID number, which allows you to set up banking and brokerage accounts. Think of lawyers as the architects who sketch out the plans for how your house will be built. This is what they do for you when you sit down with them and tell them about your plans for the fund, how the strategy will work, and where the assets will come from. The lawyer will take your ideas and put them on paper so that you can operate in a safe, legal environment and make money for you and your investors. The time it takes to complete the documents can range from a few weeks to a few months. It really depends on how much work needs to be done and how busy the lawyer and the team are when you engage their services. Remember that your first fund is the hardest one to create. However, the more you do it, the easier it becomes. You are not reinventing the wheel.

During the drafting of the documents, you need to determine which other service providers you are going to use. In most cases, the lawyers will provide you with a good reference list of firms you can work with; the prime broker will provide you with information on accountants and administrators as well. The lawyers will most likely have a preferred list of people they like dealing with for all of the functions you need. This list is usually a good place to start. Choosing the remaining service providers is important because not only is each mentioned in the documents, they also will want to review the material and provide comments. It is important to go through this step because they often add valuable information to the material.

As a case in point, most fund managers do not think that an accountant is important to the legal documents or that an administrator has anything to add, because their main jobs are to keep the books and to maintain records of the fund, respectively. Yet in reality, both can be extremely helpful in making sure the lawyer spells out in the documents the proper and most efficient way for you to charge and collect your fees. The accountant and administrator can provide significant insight into the financial structure of the fund, which in turn determines how you are paid. It is very important to have your accountant and your administrator review the materials *before* they go to press, because without a doubt, they will find an error or two in the final draft that could save you significant headaches in the future (which may include additional legal bills).

If your lawyer objects to having the accountant and administrator review the documents, then you should fire that person and find another lawyer. Several sets of eyes are important. However, once the documents have been completed, you probably will talk to your lawyer only once or twice a month. You should keep your lawyer up-to-date about the number of investors, the amount of assets in the fund, and the performance. You should also have no problem asking your lawyer or any other service provider for leads on potential investors. Service providers can be a good resource in this area. Don't discount how helpful these people can be to your organization.

PRIME BROKERS

A single manager fund cannot exist without a prime broker. This is a fact that cannot be overlooked. Without a prime broker, a fund cannot trade, make investments, or do anything to navigate the markets. That being said, in the past 10 years the prime brokerage business has really led the charge in increasing the size of the hedge fund industry. One reason that prime brokers have been responsible for growth in the industry is because they see the unique opportunity that exists in providing execution services to money managers. And even as spreads have tightened and commissions decreased, prime brokers are still pushing harder than ever because they have turned the business of executing orders into a numbers game. It is really quite simple. Essentially, the more funds they have, the more money they make. It is about quality and quantity. With the proliferation of trading technology, the costs of doing business have declined significantly, meaning that prime brokers can offer good, cheap services to basically anyone who wants them. The days of the expense of the human broker for every account are over. In most cases, human brokers have been completely taken out of the execution process, replaced instead by trading screens piped through the Internet to a fund manager. Today, with a point and click of your mouse, you can buy, sell, or borrow.

Just 10 years ago, the number of firms offering prime brokerage services to hedge funds was well under 50. Today the number is in the hundreds. It seems that with each new issue of a hedge fund newsletter or magazine, there is another story of a prime brokerage start-up firm with an exciting new take on execution services.

As a moniker, *prime broker* is a perfect description of what the firm does for the fund manager. The prime broker provides a number of services and functions to the fund that include, but are not limited to, start-up consulting, trading and execution, portfolio reporting, risk management, securities lending, office space, technology support, leverage, and capital introduction. Of course, the main business is providing a place for the manager to execute orders. The remaining services are used to entice the fund into working with the firm.

"Our role is to provide the fund manager with all the services that they need in order to operate their business and so that they can stick to picking stocks," said one prime brokerage salesperson. "We will provide them with office space, phone systems, a Bloomberg, and basically whatever they need so that they can stay focused and manage their portfolios."

It is against the law for a prime broker to require funds to trade specific amounts of shares or positions of their portfolio through it. However, the unwritten rule is that if a fund does more than 50 percent of its orders away from its prime broker, it might not be treated as well as a fund that does more than 50 percent of its orders with the firm.

"We cannot control how much or how little they do with us. But because we keep all of the records, we know how much money they are managing and get a feed at the end of the day of all the trades that were done with us and away from us [so] we know what is going on," said the prime brokerage salesperson. "If the numbers don't add up, the first thing we are going to do is ask why they are going away. And the second thing we are going to do is figure out how to get them to do more with us. If we don't get an uptick in the volume of trades, then we are going to raise their rates, which will in a nice way get them to move to another shop."

In all fairness, a prime broker should be compensated for all of the services it provides. Because of changes in soft dollars rules, the cost of doing business for hedge funds is going up. A few years ago, hedge funds could use *soft dollars,* or credits given to investment managers for paying higher commissions on their trades, for practically anything they needed. Now that is just not the case. In the fall of 2005, the Securities and Exchange Commission tightened the rules regarding what investment managers could and could not use soft dollars for in the normal course of their business.[2] As a result, fund managers are trying to minimize the costs of doing business because these costs come out of the fund and their coffers. Today, price really does matter. That is the bottom line.

Office space is one enticement for hedge fund managers that has helped a number of prime brokerage firms build very successful practices.

Prime brokers who offer office space—through vehicles that are called *hedge fund hotels*—not only charge significantly for the space and the services that come with the real estate, but also provide a real service to managers who don't want to be bothered with building out their own offices.

Managers are not forced to take the space, but they often realize that the cost of moving into a hedge fund hotel, even if only for a few years, is cheaper than going out and building their own offices.

One manager told me that she could not believe all of the headaches associated with setting up her own office. She said that if she had to do it again, she would move into her prime broker's office just for the mere fact that if something went wrong in the office she would have someone responsible to call who would most likely respond with a resolution.

In Manhattan, if you walk the blocks along Park Avenue from Grand Central Terminal to West 57th Street, you cannot throw a rock without hitting a hedge fund hotel or a stand-alone hedge fund. The city is littered with these types of operations.

However, because of the dramatic rise in the hedge fund industry, the business of offering these services has expanded to the point that Manhattan is just one of many cities where a new manager can set up shop in space controlled by a prime broker. Managers now have a choice about where to set up shop, because technology allows them to trade from nearly anywhere. Now that the option is available, many new managers are taking advantage of being outside of the major metropolitan areas.

To be clear, prime brokers do more than simply provide office space. This is something that smaller funds seem to take advantage of but that most funds of size do not. In short, they let the manager stay focused on picking stocks and implementing strategy instead of dealing with logistical issues for the business. Most prime brokers today offer online, real-time portfolio reporting, which includes position-level data and a real-time profit and loss statement. The information is just a click away and is available 24 hours a day, 365 days a year, through secured Web sites and networks. Offering this type of service is truly an amazing accomplishment for many of these firms, considering that just a few short years ago many prime brokers messengered daily reports on paper to managers a few hours after the market closed.

Most prime brokers offer some sort of portfolio accounting package that lets managers see a very real and often live picture of the status of their portfolios. They can instantaneously get fee and expense detail, along with risk reporting and leverage information.

"It is truly amazing what we can get with a click of the mouse," said Peter Cook, director of finance and administration at Dix Hills Partners, a New Jersey–based hedge fund. "Technology has leveled the playing field and now the data is readily available anytime I want it."

Some prime brokers pride themselves on the level of detail they provide clients through their reporting systems, while others focus on the type of execution provided to clients and their ability to offer "good borrows" on the short side. The landscape is truly cluttered with prime brokers, and the lines are blurred regarding who is better. In the end, it comes down to service and price.

Most managers believe that their prime broker's job is to provide the best execution possible. They believe that once that they are established they can develop their own internal capabilities to deliver the same services that prime brokers offer as an incentive to do business with them.

"We don't want a firm that offers all sorts of bells and whistles and programs that are supposed to make our business better when in turn it costs us more money to do business," said one manager who was looking for a new prime broker at the time of this writing. "We want a firm that is going to make sure our trades are done quickly and efficiently and at the cheapest cost. Bells and whistles are great, but price is what is important."

One of the new selling points that prime brokers are using to attract customers is the promise of successful capital introduction. Prime brokers are promising new and existing clients that they will be able to help them raise assets. *Capital introduction* has become the new buzz phrase in the prime brokerage industry. Everyone seems to be talking about how firms are delivering on their promises of assets. The selling point is that now managers will be able to count on their primes to help them gain access to investors who will fill their funds with cash. The reality is that because of the regulations surrounding how money is raised and who can and cannot provide this function, the promise of assets from a prime broker is often empty. It is the one thing that the prime broker rarely, if ever, is able to deliver on successfully. You should not choose a prime broker because it is offering you capital introduction services.

"Our hands are tied. We can have events. We let managers make presentations. And we can try to get the right people in the room. But it is very difficult to actually deliver in assets," said one prime brokerage employee who works in capital introduction. "Our compliance department is very strict on what we can and cannot say about a fund. They are strict about who can and cannot come to our events. Our hands are truly tied when it comes to this area of the business. We try real hard, but we are not really successful because of the limitations placed on us by the firm and the regulators."

If you believe that prime brokers will provide you with access to capital and help you bring investors to the table, I suggest you speak to other managers who use the firm for this service. In my experience, 9 times out of 10 I would expect you to find that their prime brokers did offer them some help by letting them attend and make a presentation at capital introduction events, but that the effort did not lead to enormous capital inflows. Raising money is very hard, and prime brokers offer little or no real assistance in this area.

The way to raise money is covered later in this book. Now we need to look at accounting firms and the role they will play in your organization.

ACCOUNTANTS

In my opinion, no provider is more important to the hedge fund than an audit firm. The role of the audit firm is simple: to check the firm's books and records and to authenticate the fund's track record. The role of the accountant has become increasingly important over the past few years as investors look for more detailed portfolio and fund information. Investors put a lot of weight on who the fund uses as an auditor during the due diligence process, and it is important for you to make sure you have a name brand.

"If the fund does not use an auditor that we recognize as being a firm that has experience in the hedge fund world, we will not even look twice at them," said Richard Bookbinder. "Audited financials provide a clear view into the fund and its manager, and it is a very important part of our due diligence work."

Hedge fund accounting firms charge a range of fees based on the size of the fund's assets, the number of investors, and the strategy. Funds that are harder to price than others cost more than those that trade easy-to-price securities. Similarly, if a fund is relatively small—say under $100 million in assets under management—it most likely will pay less than $50,000 for audit and tax work, while very large funds often pay significantly higher fees that sometimes reach multiples of what the smaller funds pay.

"It all depends on the scope of the work," said Peter Testaverde, the partner in charge of the hedge fund practice at Goldstein Golub Kessler LLC.

As the number of funds has grown, so has the number of firms seeking audits. In turn, this has put significant pressure on accounting firms. Today most of the Big Four firms will not accept new clients unless they come from an existing shop or with a recommendation from high atop the mountain. This was not the case a few years ago, when everyone in the industry was trying to poach everyone else's clients. Currently, the Big Four are pushed to capacity, and the second tier or regional firms are also feeling pressure. As a result, a huge opportunity for smaller, more local firms has emerged, and those who are trying to build this area of their practice are seeing extremely good results in new business growth. With the problem of too much work for firms, another pressure point is emerging in the industry—the poaching of talent. As more and more funds are being regulated and registered, they are looking for experienced financial people to run this side of their business. This, in conjunction with firms being pushed to the max, is causing real stress on the hedge fund accounting industry. The poaching of people is causing a number of firms to see a lot of good people—partners in some cases—jumping ship to clients and competitors.

"As hedge funds continue to grow, they look for talent that they can bring in-house that allows them to continue to grow and expand and use their outside service providers better," said Testaverde. "We see a lot of good people—not just from our firm but from around the industry—who have decided to go inside. It is a win-win for both the fund and the individual, because the fund gets a good person on the inside who will work hard and the accountant gets a really unique opportunity to put their skills to work in a totally different environment and reap the benefits that come with working for a large hedge fund. The CPA firms are the only losers because a lot of good talent is walking out the door into the clients' offices."

The issue for the new fund manager is how to keep track of the books and records and track data accordingly. The answer is that when a new fund is launched, it must keep thorough records of all money flows and transactions. Most of the data for this can be compiled from customer records and brokerage statements. The structure of the fund will determine how fees are calculated and paid and how expenses will be accrued and defined in the offering memorandum. The accountant will use the offering memorandum as the road map to determine how to allocate profits and losses to investors and fees to the manager.

When it comes to running the day-to-day and month-to-month accounting functions of your business, you have two choices: You can do it internally or externally. Most of the back-office functions associated with the fund can be found on the prime brokerage reporting system, which makes the job of the in-house accountant that much easier. You can also outsource this function of your business to a third party, who will keep track of the data and provide you with performance and accounting information—this is the role of the administrator. Keeping it inside has benefits, as does outsourcing the functions. The question is, what are your company's abilities and resources? Benefits of having an internal person include the speed with which performance data is prepared and the fact that he or she can sometimes help with risk management by providing financial insight into the portfolio. If the in-house accountant has a background in audit and tax, this can also reduce the workload of the outside CPA firm. Regardless of which you choose, remember that even if you have an in-house person with audit and tax experience, you are still going to need to hire a third-party firm to prepare the audit. It is important to sit down with your accounting people and learn how management and incentive fees are to be calculated and how they will deal with high-water marks, realized gains and losses, interest income, loss carryforwards, and hot issues. You need to calculate and monitor these things on a monthly basis. It is important that you know how these items are accounted for and calculated so you understand the fund's financial position at all times.

Choosing an audit firm is as difficult as choosing any other service provider. However, with an auditor, there is a lot less hullabaloo. In the end, the numbers never lie, and an auditor's work is completely objective. Like law firms, many CPA firms introduce you to the partner and then hand off the work to an associate or junior-level staffer. It is mission critical that when you meet with your accountant, you find out who is actually going to do the work on your fund. You need to meet with that person to make sure you believe in his or her ability to get the job done. Once again, remember that you are the client and have a right to ask questions and get answers.

Most CPA firms have knowledgeable staff at all levels of the organization. However, it is important to understand how many people they have dedicated to the hedge fund practice, what sort of clients they have, and what services they can provide to make your operation run more efficiently. The fewer the people, the less of a commitment they may have to the hedge fund industry and in turn to your work. Check their references, but remember that very few people provide references unless they know how those references will respond to the questions that you are going to ask. Most references offer little or no insight into the organization or its skills. The key is to ask clients about the services you are expecting to receive from the firm and try to get an understanding of how it performs the tasks you need for your fund. A firm may be good in one area and weak in another; you need to understand this before signing on. Changing auditors is not something that investors or potential investors take lightly, as it poses potential problems. Therefore, it is mission critical to get it right the first time.

ADMINISTRATORS

Over the past few years, a number of onshore funds have started using third-party administrators to provide many of the day-to-day and monthly functions that in-house accountants often do. Just as auditors provide an objective accounting of the fund's finances through the yearly audit, the administrator can also provide objective accounting services, such as net asset value calculations and capital inflows and outflows, to allow for a more thorough and complete look at the fund and its finances on a monthly basis.

Hedge fund administrators who operate onshore provide similar services to those of transfer agents and custodians in the mutual fund business. The reason most onshore, single-strategy managers use administrators is that they can't afford to have an in-house team of accountants to handle this function, and the use of an administrator is a cost-effective and reliable solution. Most administrators charge a declining basis point fee based on assets under management. Some will charge a flat monthly fee in the beginning and go to the sliding scale once the fund ramps up its operation.

Due to the structure of offshore funds, it is an entity unto itself that simply employs the manager and has an independent board of directors and investors. It needs an administrator to keep track of not only asset flows and trading data but also client information. In the wake of the

World Trade Center disaster, some administrators provide anti–money laundering services to funds to ensure that they are in compliance with the new rules resulting from the USA Patriot Act.

The use of an administrator is much more prevalent among offshore single-fund managers than it is within the United States, because administrator services are also sometimes provided by onshore prime brokers. The difference between onshore and offshore structures is covered in Chapter 3.

The use of administrators is most prevalent in the fund of funds industry. These managers use an administrator to keep their books and records and to track their positions in the underlying funds. Funds of funds usually do not have a prime broker and simply operate with a bank account that investor assets flow in and out of and a bank account that handles the operating expenses. Because they do not have a brokerage account to keep track of their positions, they use an administrator to fill this void. The administrator tracks the underlying fund positions and provides reports on how the fund and its funds are doing.

Over the next few years, I believe that as the fund industry continues to grow, the administration side of the business will grow along with it. In some cases, having an administrator makes a fund seem more professional, and currently that is what a lot of funds need to raise assets.

MARKETING AND MARKETERS

Ultimately, the hardest part of the money management business is raising money. The second hardest part is managing it. Don't let anyone fool you. There are plenty of people out there who say that picking the right stocks or choosing the right bonds is the hardest thing a manager is faced with. But in reality, raising money is a lot harder than either of those tasks.

To understand how to manage money you have to do the following: Read a book about value investing, study the principles of Graham and Dodd, follow the thoughts of Warren Buffett and Charlie Munger in any of the Berkshire Hathaway annual reports, and read articles about George Soros, Julian Robertson, and Michael Steinhardt, and you will get an instant education on how to do it. All of this material will tell you basically the same thing, which is to find things that are cheap, load up your truck, and sell the investments when they are no longer cheap. You don't need to be a chartered financial analyst or a Harvard MBA to be a good investor. You just need to understand how to identify good companies at reasonable prices. It is not rocket science, and anyone who suggests otherwise is lying. The idea that only CFAs or MBAs are qualified to manage money is insane.

However, I believe that marketing or asset raising is a unique science. At any given moment, somebody somewhere is trying to sell you something. The problem is that they may not know what they are doing, they may be speaking to the wrong person, or they simply may not be very good at what they do and will therefore fail. As the hedge fund industry has grown over the past few years, it has attracted a number of people who specialize in marketing or asset raising who I would say have little or no business being in this business. You need to be careful of these people, because they will not help your business. On the contrary, they will just hurt it. The reason is that everyone thinks that they can market; they think they know what to do and believe that they will be successful. My friends, most times they fail and fall flat on their faces.

As a budding hedge fund manager, you need to understand that raising money is going to be hard. While the press writes about a fund that launched with $500 million or another fund that launched with a couple of billion dollars, this is not the day-to-day reality. Very few funds launch with substantial assets. You need to understand this, because without capital, you do not have a business. In order to avoid the pitfalls that many new funds make, you need to be cognizant of one important rule: The only people who will be able to raise assets for you are people who are as committed to the business as you are. These individuals are very difficult to find.

For the most part, marketing or salespeople are thought of as the knuckle draggers on Wall Street. It is assumed that they don't understand how to put on a trade or how to execute an order, so they are put into the asset-raising side of the business, where the good times roll. This is total and utter nonsense. Marketers are the front line. They are your eyes and ears on the Street, as well as the first people most potential investors come in contact with when they learn about your firm. It is vital that you realize just how important these people are to you and your organization. They are the gasoline that makes the engine run.

Going out and asking for $1 million, $10 million, or $100 million is a lot harder than looking at a screen and deciding to buy $1 million, $10 million, or a $100 million in shares of stock. For many successful managers, there is little or no emotion in actual trading, whereas there is an enormous amount of emotion in asking someone to invest in a fund. If you don't believe this, try it, and you will see firsthand that what I am saying is the truth.

In building a successful hedge fund, you need to identify the roles that you and your partners are going to play. Someone needs to be responsible for managing the money. Someone needs to be responsible for the back office. And a third person needs to be responsible for marketing and client relations. If there are only two of you in the beginning, it make sense to divvy up the tasks according to your individual strengths. This is often the easiest part of the exercise, because then you need to make sure that each of you follows through. Initially, when it comes to marketing you need to make sure that you have the right message and that the material puts forth exactly what you want to say about the fund and your strategy.

Marketing 101 and 102 are covered in Chapter 6, but for now think of it this way: Every time you make your pitch, you should make sure that you communicate a clear and concise message about your fund to the prospect. Provide ample time for your prospects to ask questions. Remember, if you don't have the answer, tell them that you don't know and will get back to them. Never try to fake it. Believe me, this will cost you. Whether you think the investor is sophisticated or not, he or she will see right through you and it will cause you to lose the sale. And you need to make sales to raise money.

For the most part, the days of raising money by taking people out for dinner and drinks or a round of golf are over. Now investors are demanding more information about the funds, the managers, and the people in the organization. People don't want to get caught with their pants down if and when the fund blows up. Therefore, investors are collecting more and more data on funds. It is all in an attempt to do thorough due diligence. It is questionable how thorough this due diligence can be in light of the situation surrounding Bayou and other fraudulent funds. Some very well respected and sophisticated investors found themselves caught in this web of deceit. Ultimately, this has forced legitimate marketers to work that much harder to provide potential investors with information for the due diligence process.

Marketers need to be smart, aggressive, forward-thinking people who understand that raising money is a numbers game. The more people you get in front of, the more people who potentially will invest. If you sit in the office and wait for investors to call, you will be sitting for a very long time waiting for something that will never happen.

CHAPTER 3

Hedge Fund Structures

L aunching a hedge fund is both easy and difficult. It is easy because the process is rather simple: You hire a lawyer to write the documents, you open a prime brokerage account, you get some investors, and you are off. The whole process can take as little as 90 to 120 days. Yet launching a hedge is difficult because of all the nuances that need to be addressed with the lawyer, prime broker, auditor, administrator, and investors.

Very few funds launch on time and without a hitch. There are many moving pieces that go into a successful launch. The key is to pay attention to all aspects of the launch to ensure success and not waste time.

This chapter is dedicated to hedge fund structures. It explains the role of the lawyer, accountant, and administrator during the initial phase of your operation and details how hedge funds go from an idea in the manager's head to the reality of being an investment vehicle.

GETTING STARTED

When launching your fund, you first need to determine where your investors will be based and what types of assets they will invest with you. The answers will put in place the foundation of the structure that the lawyer will create. In the beginning, most start-ups get assets from friends and family and, consequently, create U.S.-domiciled entities that are able to accept taxable assets. However, if the manager has a commitment for assets from investors outside of the United States, tax-exempt U.S. investors, or both, it might make sense to launch an offshore fund first and follow with an onshore fund.

The structure and its domicile is dictated by the flow of investor assets. Most U.S.-based managers start with an onshore fund simply because it is where they can invest their money and where they can accept money from friends and family.

As discussed previously, the structure du jour is a Delaware-based limited liability company. Most lawyers believe that this type of structure provides managers with the best vehicle to operate and run their business. As the regulatory environment evolves and continues to change, the structure of choice may change as well. From the late 1940s until just a few years ago, the structure of choice was the limited partnership. Whatever structure you choose, there is one thing that I can promise you: Your lawyer will ensure that as long as you do not commit fraud or do anything illegal, it will be extremely hard for you or any of your colleagues to be personally liable should something go wrong and the fund blow up. In either a limited partnership or a limited liability company structure, it is very difficult for disgruntled investors to pierce the corporate veil. This means that should all hell break loose, you should be protected on a personal level. However, if you commit fraud, all bets are off, and nothing will save you from your actions. In this case, all hell breaking loose means that a fund does not perform well. This is not something that most new managers and their lawyers like to talk about, because everyone who launches believes he or she is going to be the next George Soros or Julian Robertson. However, this not the reality, and it is important for you and your partners to know that this sort of protection exists. This is why you can't go to a local lawyer who has no experience in setting up funds. You need to go to someone who specializes in hedge funds, understands the issues, and knows what is important to include in the document to make sure you are protected and that you and your investors are treated fairly.

"Doing documents is not that hard," said one hedge fund lawyer. "Most of the big firms in the city have some sort of hedge fund practice, and there are a number of firms that do only hedge fund work. The key is to have someone who knows about the industry, so that the manager gets a document that is similar to others that their investors see and has all of the protections that are needed should something go wrong and an investor sues."

When it comes to setting up a hedge fund, you can either go with an onshore vehicle, an offshore vehicle, or both. As I mentioned, the domicile you choose will be a function of asset flows. Onshore funds are for the most part domiciled in Delaware because of that state's pro-business laws. Offshore funds are domiciled in tax-haven jurisdictions such as the Cayman Islands, Bermuda, and the British Virgin Islands (BVI). Along with the two types of funds, there are three types of investors: domestic taxable investors, domestic tax-exempt investors, and nontaxable offshore investors. *Domestic taxable investors* are investors who have to pay tax on profits they make from their investments. For the most part, this group includes individuals and for-profit institutions that are based in the United States and pay tax on their worldwide income. *Domestic nontaxable investors* include, but are not limited to, pension plans, endowments, and charitable foundations and trusts that are the retirement accounts of domestic taxable investors. These investors are domiciled here in the United States but because of their tax status do not pay income tax. The third group of investors, *nontaxable offshore investors,* includes any individual or institution that is not based in the United States and therefore does not have to pay tax to the Internal Revenue Service.

The key to a successful launch is to understand what type of investors you will have and where the assets you will attract are coming from. By doing so, you will be able to make sure that you have the right vehicle for the money. The last thing you want to deal with are investors who wish to invest with you but cannot because you don't have the right vehicle for their assets.

In some cases, particularly with offshore investors, location, rather than structure, is important, and this dictates whether they will invest in a fund. For example, if you are marketing to Japanese investors, it is mission critical that you have a Cayman-based unit trust. This group of investors rarely, if ever, invests in a hedge fund that is not set up as a unit trust. Therefore, if you discuss another corporation based in a different tax-haven jurisdiction, these investors will most likely decline, because they don't approve of the fund's structure and domicile. It does not matter if they agree with the fund's strategy and like the fund's manager. They simply will not invest because of the structure and the domicile.

Similarly, you cannot take Delaware-based LLCs to Boston-based nonprofits, because they cannot invest in an onshore without a potential problem from the Internal Revenue Service.

The point is to know your market. Understand your investors' needs before you bring them a product. Make sure that you can get over the simplest objections during the courting process.

Today, in the fall of 2006, domestic hedge funds are usually set up as limited liability companies. Rarely, if ever, are S or C corporations used for these types of investment vehicles. The structure outlined here includes both an entity for the management of the fund and an entity in which the assets are managed.

The typical fund complex structure consists of two groups: (1) the *members* (i.e., the investors in the fund) and (2) the *managing member* (i.e., the management company or the manager). The managing member is the entity that provides investment management and runs the day-to-day administrative functions of the organization. The members are the investors who provide the capital that the managing member invests. The members, or investors, have "an economic interest" in the fund equal to their investment, and they share in the fund's profits and losses. Their liability is limited to the amount of their investment in the fund. In short, they can lose only as much as they have invested and nothing more than their initial investment.

The managing member, or manager, charges the members a management and an incentive, or performance, fee. The management fee, which currently ranges from 1 to 2 percent of assets under management, is calculated on the net assets of the fund and is usually paid to the managing member quarterly. The managing member also charges an incentive fee, usually 20 percent of the profits earned on the portfolio. This fee is usually calculated quarterly and paid annually to the management company. The incentive fee is calculated based on the profits of the fund and is something that aligns the hedge fund manager's interests to the investors' interest. If the fund and, in turn, the investors make money, the manager makes money. If the fund does not make money, then the manager does not make money, other than his or her management fee.

Most hedge funds employ something called a *high-water mark,* which is used when calculating the manager's incentive fee. Should a fund lose money in any given period, the manager must earn back the losses that were incurred—back to the point of zero losses, or the high-water mark—before being able to charge an incentive fee. Most managers who have a high-water mark in place take their performance allocation yearly, because they do not want to have to pay back any fees earned and received should they experience losses later in the year.

All of this will be explained and set forth in your initial meetings with the lawyer and accountant. How fees are paid and accounted for will be explained in the fund's documents. The private placement memorandum, or offering documents, provides a very thorough explanation of how the fund is to be operated, managed, and administered. It details all of the risks, both potential and real, that investors are exposing themselves to by investing with the manager. It also provides significant insight into the fund's legal structure, investment style and strategy, management and operation team, investment and redemption policies, and tax issues.

Most documents spell out so many risks for potential for loss that if investors truly believed what they read, they would be considered crazy for investing in the fund. "The idea is cover all of the bases," said a hedge fund lawyer. "Our job is really to protect our clients from any and all litigation by putting in so many risks, explaining the risks thoroughly, and then having the investors sign off that they have read the documents in their subscription documents. We are providing a certain level of protection to the investment manager."

THE SETUP

From a mechanical perspective, setting up a hedge fund is the same as launching any new business. Your lawyer will file a certificate of formation with the domiciled state that creates the entity in which the fund operates. You will request a tax identification number from the Internal Revenue Service. And you will need to open two bank accounts. One of the accounts will be used for the day-to-day operational expenses of the organization, and the other will be used as a conduit for investors in which to accept and redeem their investments. It is important to keep these two accounts separate. I am of the opinion that you never want to be in the situation where you are commingling client assets with operational monies. This could lead to a real nightmare, and it is good to avoid nightmares.

To accept investors, you will need to provide them with three things: (1) the private placement memorandum, (2) the subscription documents, and (3) the operating agreement of the limited liability company. In some cases, the subscription document and operating agreements are combined into one package, but they are two very different documents. As I discuss in Chapter 6, the idea is to keep it simple. To do this, you must know all aspects of the documents so you can answer any question that arises, or at least know where the question is addressed in the documents. I do not believe it is necessary for you to memorize the material. That would be a brutal exercise. However, you should become very familiar with the contents and makeup of the material. I advise all of my clients to study the documents, question their lawyers about the contents, and really try to understand them. Being prepared will allow you to succeed.

The process for investment is simple. Once investors are deemed qualified, they enter into an agreement with the hedge fund to have their money managed. The document that details this is called the *limited liability company operating agreement* for domestic funds (onshore investors) and the *articles of incorporation* for offshore funds (offshore investors). At the same time that investors are completing the operating agreement, they also fill out a subscription agreement.

The subscription agreement details the amount and type of investment they are making in the fund. Along with detailing the investor's investment, the subscription agreement also is used by the manager to collect background information on the investor so that the fund and/or its administrator can perform know-your-customer (KYC) and anti–money laundering (AML) functions that are currently required. (KYC and AML issues, strategies, and practices are discussed in the Chapter 6.) Consequently, the subscription document is used to collect Social Security numbers or tax identification numbers, addresses, phone numbers, investment history, marital status, and employment status. The subscription document should be viewed as a tool to learn more about your investors—their account application, if you will. The information is quite basic, but it is important to collect. In light of the events of September 11, 2001, the U.S. government has become very focused on money laundering, in particular as related to terrorism activities. The government and its agencies require managers to ensure to the best of their ability that their investors are not using the hedge fund as a tool to launder money. The government takes this issue very seriously. Make sure that when you discuss accepting investors with your lawyer, you ask questions about KYC and AML rules and the regulations that you are required to fulfill to be compliant. This is something you do not want to overlook. Following is a brief story to prove my point and to open your eyes to how serious an issue this is.

A few years ago, a Justice Department employee was speaking at a hedge fund conference about how the government was reacting to the money laundering problems uncovered in light of the attacks of September 11. After his speech, a hedge fund manager raised his hand and asked, "How serious is the government about money laundering?" Without missing a beat, the speaker replied, "How does 10 to 20 years sound?" The audience was in shock. Money laundering is a serious issue, and something you as a hedge fund manager need to be cognizant of regardless of how small or insular you think your investor base may be. AML rules and regulations are discussed later in this chapter.

As described, the management company or managing member is the entity responsible for all aspects of the operation of the fund. In this capacity, it will manage and operate the fund and be paid a management fee for its services. The fund uses a management company to manage and operate the fund, rather than employing people directly, to avoid potential liabilities.

In theory, this structure shields the management team from liability should something go wrong with the fund. Of course, there are limits to the strength of the shield (e.g., if the manager commits fraud or breaks the law). In the most basic definition, *fraud* occurs when the manager steals the fund's money to buy a new car or pay off another investor in a Ponzi scheme; *lawbreaking* occurs when the manager trades on insider information or engages in front running a position. In front running, a manager sells or buys a security for his or her own account *before* filling orders from the fund, thereby taking advantage of the upward price movement that the second order causes. In either case, the limited liability company will not shield the manager and its employees from the investor and/or regulator litigation. The limited liability company will shield the manager and its employees should the strategy fail or the market crash and the fund's assets go to zero.

In today's litigious society, lawyers representing investors are working very hard to pierce the corporate veil protecting managers and their teams from personal liability. A true test of this will be the outcome of the litigation surrounding the massive fraud that the world knows as the Bayou hedge fund case.

The Bayou class action suit was filed in November 2005 by investors who believed that they were defrauded by the fund and its managers. The suit alleges that ever since the funds were launched in 1996, the managers operated a "financial sham and Ponzi scheme" in which defendants, two of Bayou's principals, and others fraudulently induced investors to invest approximately $450 million in the Bayou Hedge Funds.

The suit further alleges that the principals of the fund spent the investors' money on luxury homes and cars rather than actually investing in the assets as per the fund documents.[1]

On September 29, 2005, Bayou's founder, Samuel Israel III, and its chief financial officer, Daniel E. Marino, pleaded guilty to charges that they stole more than $450 million from investors. Israel, 46, pleaded guilty to three counts of conspiracy, mail fraud, and investment advisory fraud. He faces up to 30 years in prison and fines of up to $250,000 for each count. Marino pleaded guilty to one count of conspiracy and three counts of fraud. He faces up to 50 years in prison and fines of up to $250,000 per count.[2] The two men were to be sentenced in mid-2006.

Along with Israel and Marino, the class action suit names Citibank, NA, two of the Hennessee Group LLC's principals, and Sterling Stamos Capital Management, LP as defendants. According to the suit, Citibank facilitated the fraud by permitting Israel to transfer at least $120 million of the investors' assets to his personal bank accounts. The suit further alleges that the Hennessee Group and Sterling Stamos Capital Management did not conduct appropriate due diligence on the Bayou funds before they recommended them to clients as sound investments.[3]

The suit also alleges that the defendants failed to monitor the funds and provide up-to-date reports on their activities. An interesting twist to the suit is that the plaintiffs' law firm, Berger & Montague PC, is trying to pierce the corporate veil of the Hennessee Group by naming the husband-and-wife team of Charles J. Gradante and E. Lee Hennessee as alter egos to the company.[4] If the lawsuit is successful, Gradante and Hennessee will be held personally liable for their actions, along with their firm. According to a number of lawyers with whom I spoke regarding this specific aspect of the suit, it will be very difficult for the plaintiffs' lawyer to successfully prove the "alter ego" charges, but if they do it will most likely set a precedent in the hedge fund industry.

Regardless of the outcome of the class action suit, hedge fund lawyers will continue to construct organizations that limit the manager's personal liability. Your lawyer will create a web of entities that should shield you, your colleagues, and your assets from litigation. Figure 3.1 is a diagram of the most commonly used onshore structure.

Prior to the National Securities Markets Improvement Act of 1996, all hedge funds were limited to 100 investors. This meant that once the 100 investor slots were filled, the manager had to turn investors away. Prior to the changes in the law, there really was very little chance of maneuvering around this issue. Some managers simply cloned their funds to accept more investors, but this was deemed in violation of the Investment Company Act of 1940. As a result, it forced fund managers to register the products as mutual funds if they exceeded the 100-investor limit. This was not an option. One way many managers sidestepped the issue was to create new funds that incorporated a variation of how the old fund operated or was managed. In some cases, the managers would create funds that had longer lockups, used

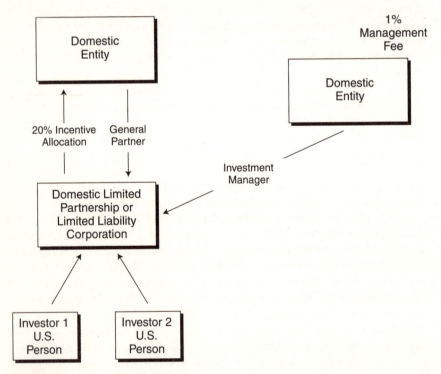

FIGURE 3.1 Simple Onshore Structure
Source: Created and reprinted by permission of Maury Cartine, JD, CPA.

more leverage, and used private equity investments to differentiate one fund from another. Tiger Management, led by Julian Robertson, was famous for coming up with new ways to skin this cat! Robertson and his team were instrumental in working with the people in Washington, D.C., to update the rules regarding investors.

The National Market Improvement Act of 1996 changed the rules of the game by implementing Section 3(c)(7), which allows managers to set up funds that can accept as many as 500 investors, as long as all of the investors are deemed to be qualified purchasers. A *qualified purchaser* is defined as an individual or family company having at least $5 million in investment assets or a company that owns or manages at least $25 million in investment assets.[5]

The 3(c)(7) fund, as it is called in the industry, provides managers with a significant amount of latitude in how to build their businesses. Prior to 1997, managers with 100 investors had to close their doors to new investors and were able to build their businesses organically only through their existing client base.

Today, a manager who can attract institutional assets, which may include funds of funds, can build quite a significant business through the use of a 3(c)(7) fund. However, there is one sticking point: A manager cannot simply convert his or her 3(c)(1) fund—the traditional 100-investor vehicle—to a 3(c)(7) simply to let in more investors. Furthermore, a 3(c)(7) cannot accept accredited investors; it is open only to qualified purchasers. Managers are not allowed to run a version of the 3(c)(1) fund as a 3(c)(7) in an attempt to be open to more investors. For everything to be acceptable to the regulators, there must be two different funds that are managed distinctly.

"The funds can be similar, but they must be different," said a hedge fund attorney. "The regulators gave managers a little when they allowed for the new structure, but they did not make it easy for them. In some cases, managers are forced to make the decision to get rid of clients in order to grow or to not grow. Whichever structure the manager chooses, [he or she is] limited in some way to the number of investors and who is able to invest with them."

The sections of the Investment Company Act that exempt hedge fund managers from registering are Sections 3(c)(1) and 3(c)(7). To qualify for a 3(c)(1) exemption, the fund cannot accept more than 100 investors and it cannot make a public offering.[6] The fund is open to both accredited investors and up to 35 nonaccredited investors. Most fund managers do not accept nonaccredited investors for the simple reason that by doing so, they limit the growth they can experience over the lifetime of the fund. And if they do accept these nonaccredited investors, they are subject to additional disclosure requirements. However, it is sometimes necessary for funds to accept nonaccredited investors specifically from a marketing point of view.

It is very important that the investment team has some, if not all, of its net worth invested in the fund. In some cases, this poses a problem if some of team members have not yet reached the level of accredited investors; they still need to invest. The reason for this is discussed in Chapter 4. For now, it is important to understand that the only nonaccredited investors you should let into your fund are your employees. A full definition of an *accredited investor* can be found in the appendix.

When it comes to being exempt from the Investment Company Act, the Securities and Exchange Commission is very strict about how investors are counted. It uses a tool called a *look-through provision* to make sure that a fund does not accept more than 100 investors and that no investors being counted as together are counted individually. If an entity is formed for the sole purpose of investing in a single hedge fund or fund of funds and therefore is investing more than 10 percent of its assets in one manager, the SEC says that all of the individuals who form the entity must be counted as individual investors in the fund in which they are investing. This means that if 10 people get together and each invest $100,000 in a partnership, then take that $1 million and invest it into Fund FLJ, the manager of Fund FLJ needs to count the investment as coming from 10 individual investors. Since it takes 10 slots and is a relatively small amount of money, the manager's ability to grow will be stunted.

The SEC uses two tests to determine whether the look-through position applies. The first test is whether more than 10 percent of assets are invested in a single fund. The second test is whether more than 10 percent of the fund's assets are invested in funds and companies that otherwise would have to register as investment companies if not for exemptions from the provisions of 3(c)(1) and 3(c)(7).

As part of adhering to federal regulations, fund managers are required to make a number of state filings when and if accepting investors from specific states. In some cases, hedge funds are required to file before accepting investor assets in a specific state; in other cases, they have to file after accepting investors from a specific state; in some cases, no filing is necessary. In some cases, filing is required when simply setting up shop. Known as *blue-sky provisions,* the filings allow the manager to do business—in other words, accept investors—and must be heeded. Initially, you should determine which states your investors are coming from and then have your lawyer make sure you are registered in these specific states either prior to or after you make the offering to the potential investors. Keeping track of blue-sky laws is a necessary evil of being in the hedge fund business and something that you and your partners need to pay close attention to when you are launching and operating your fund.

Due to the structure and nature of offshore funds, managers do not have to worry about many of the issues that arise with onshore vehicles.

However, they do need to pay attention to jurisdictional and tax issues specific to tax-exempt U.S. investors. One of the biggest concerns is anti–money laundering issues.

AML AND KYC

The USA Patriot Act is intended to prevent and detect money laundering and funding of terrorist activities. As a consequence, it creates significant compliance burdens for hedge fund managers. Title III of the Patriot Act includes two provisions that need to be addressed by hedge fund managers and their employees: (1) Section 352, which requires the establishment of an anti–money laundering program and (2) Section 326, which mandates verification of account-holder identity.[7]

Section 352 of the Patriot Act requires unregistered investment companies, including hedge funds, venture capital funds, and private equity funds to establish anti–money laundering programs if the investment vehicle permits an investor to redeem any portion of the investor's interest within two years of purchase.[8] The idea is that Congress believes that illiquid investments are usually less useful to money launderers. Because a typical private equity or venture capital fund does not permit investors to redeem any portion of their interests within two years of purchase, these types of funds are not required to adopt an anti–money laundering program under Section 352.[9]

Hedge funds without two-year lockups are deemed to be liquid investments and therefore are required to adopt AML rules and practices. Consequently, managers who are subject to Section 352 of the rule are required, at minimum, to do the following in order to guard against money laundering:

- Develop internal policies, procedures, and controls.
- Designate a compliance officer.
- Offer an ongoing employee training program.
- Arrange for an independent audit function to test programs.[10]

In addition to these procedures and tasks, hedge fund managers must also attend to Section 326 of the Act: "Verification of Identification." Under this section, the secretary of the Treasury sets forth regulations that define the minimum standards that managers have to use when identifying their customer or investors. These include the following:

- Verifying the identity of any person seeking to invest in the fund
- Maintaining records of the information used to verify the investor's identity including name, address, and other identifying information

- Consulting lists of known or suspected terrorists or terrorist organizations provided to the hedge fund by any government agency to determine whether the investor is on the list[11]

According to Carl Fornaris, an attorney who specializes in the Patriot Act at Greenburg Traurig LLP in Miami, hedge funds that are subject to the Section 352 rule are required to develop and implement written anti–money laundering programs that are approved by the fund's general partner. Offshore managers are not exempt from the Patriot Act and are required to have AML policies and procedures in place that are followed and executed at all times. Due to the heightened awareness of money laundering and financial crimes, it is very important to pay attention to AML and KYC issues, and it is important to realize that Congress has the ability to change and amend the rules and regulations at any time. Therefore, it is important for you to be in touch with your lawyer on this issue with some regularity. Read the e-mail missives that come from most lawyers every time a change or addition is made to the regulation; don't dismiss the correspondence as spam. Both on- and offshore fund managers are required to pay attention to the AML issues as long as they are based in the United States. Knowing what and what not to pay attention to will be one of the keys to your success.

Your lawyer should be able to provide you with all the counsel you need in this area. However, it is important that you take some initiative and learn the rules and regulations. For example, offshore funds are not subject to the regulations of the Investment Company Act of 1940 or those of the Commodity Futures Trading Commission. However, managers of offshore funds do need to pay specific attention to make sure that they do not run afoul of any U.S. regulations and that they observe the rules and regulations of the nation in which they are operating their fund.

Once again, the domicile of your fund will depend on whether you plan to market your fund abroad or are just looking to attract tax-exempt, onshore U.S. investors. There are specific issues regarding tax-exempt onshore investors that need to be addressed, and you need to pay attention to them. These are addressed in Chapter 4.

Most offshore investors do not care where the fund is domiciled as long as the location is deemed a tax-haven jurisdiction. If you want to grow your offshore operation, you will need to please U.S.-based investors who seek anonymity and who wish to avoid the U.S. government seeing their investments.

When you launch a fund, you need to keep this in mind in order to limit the obvious objections that will come up during the investor courting period. Never do you want to sit with potential investors and have them tell you that they like your strategy but are unable to invest with you because you do not have the right structure in the right location.

The key to successful fund-raising is to know your customer. And, while marketing is discussed in Chapter 6, it is important to think about your marketing effort during the setup and initial stages of your organization. By doing so, you will avoid embarrassing moments with potential investors.

Due to potential tax implications, nontaxable U.S. investors, such as pension plans, endowments, and charitable trusts, are required to invest mostly in offshore funds. This is because these types of investors need to avoid unrelated business taxable income, or UBTI.

If a hedge fund employs leverage to a U.S.-based tax-exempt investor, the investor would be subject to UBTI, because the Internal Revenue Service deems it to be in "a trader business." Because the fund is a flow-through entity, any income is now subject to UBTI, as per the Schedule K-1 tax form that the fund issues at the end of the year. The firm's auditor sends a K-1 form to all investors stating their profits and losses for the previous tax year as well as the investor's balance in the capital account at year-end.

"While the government does not come right out and say it, they do not want people who are not paying taxes to be in business, per se," said one accountant, who requested anonymity. "Therefore, if the IRS sees a tax-exempt investor investing in an onshore fund, they deem them to be in a business and not a not-for-profit entity. Therefore, the investor is now subject to UBTI, no different than a for-profit entity."

Most offshore funds are set up as corporations or non-flow-through entities to allow for U.S. investors who are concerned with UBTI. This means that the fund does not issue a K-1 and that the investors are not deemed to be in business. Rather, they simply have a passive investment in a company that is located in a tax-haven jurisdiction such as the Cayman Islands, Bermuda, or the British Virgin Islands and therefore are not subject to tax. The investment is viewed no as different from one in a publicly traded company here in the United States.

"By having an offshore fund, the fund manager provides the not-for-profit investor with an ability to make a passive investment in a company that happens to invest in the markets instead of making widgets," said the accountant.

The hedge fund industry in the United States and Europe is littered with service providers. The same can be said for tax-haven jurisdictions. Today, there are few problems with setting up offshore funds in these locales because it has become such an important piece of the corporate infrastructure in many of these countries.

"The hedge fund industry accounts [are] significant to the overall economy of the many places like Cayman, the BVI, and Bermuda," said Mark

Lewis, a senior partner in charge of investment funds at Walkers, a Cayman-based law firm. "The governments of these jurisdictions are very supportive of what we are doing and of the industry and have helped make it easier for us to grow and develop this area of our practice because of the vital role it plays in the community and the country's economy."

Despite significant setbacks caused by Hurricane Ivan in 2004, the hedge fund industry in the Cayman Islands has grown significantly. One reason is the perceived level of service that the island nation offers fund managers, as well as the view of many onshore lawyers that regulations are more favorable to managers than in other tax-haven jurisdictions. In 2005, 1,752 funds registered with the Cayman Islands Monetary Authority, and through June 30, 2006, more than 1,015 fund had registered in the offshore jurisdiction. These new fund launches translate into significant amounts of fees and revenue, not only for the government and its agencies, but for all of the service providers that handle hedge fund operations in Cayman and abroad. Many people and organizations are willing to guide you through offshore fund development and operation. As the customer, you should demand to receive excellent service, regardless of the size of your operation.

Most new hedge fund managers rely too heavily on their onshore counsel to direct their offshore operation. My suggestion is that you try to connect directly with offshore counsel. In most situations, hedge fund managers delegate to their onshore counsel the responsibility of finding offshore counsel. The appendix contains a listing of offshore lawyers. Contact them directly once you decide to go this route. It will save you money, time, and aggravation down the road and will give you a direct connection to this aspect of your business.

Figure 3.2 illustrates a straight-line onshore fund. It is a diagram that outlines a master-feeder structure. There is some debate among lawyers and accountants about the benefits of the master-feeder versus a structure called a side-by-side, a diagram of which also follows. However, most start-up managers use the master-feeder structure because it is easier to manage and allocate fund assets to. There are a few accounting issues with the master-feeder structure that some consider to be an irritant; however, they are not so onerous that they make the structure unworthy. More important, should you choose this structure, you are not the first and will not be the last manager to use it. Therefore, you should be able to get significant support for and resolution of any questions or issues that arise from the use of the master-feeder structure.

Many managers like the master-feeder structure because it allows them to accommodate both onshore and offshore investors through a single entity. The master-feeder structure employs a simple concept, which allows managers to accept on- and offshore assets from their respective investors,

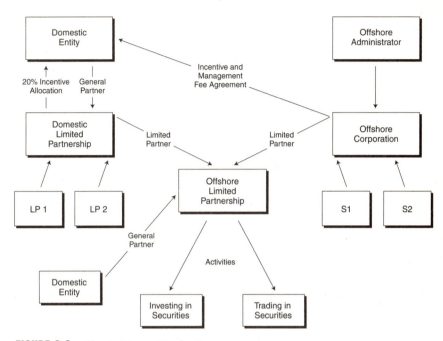

FIGURE 3.2 Classic Master-Feeder Structure
Source: Created and reprinted by permission of Maury Cartine, JD, CPA.

after which the assets are pooled into one account and managed as a single portfolio. The assets are traded in one vehicle, and the profits and losses are allocated pro rata based on where the money comes from. There are a number of benefits to the master-feeder structure. Cost is one of the most significant savings to managing the portfolio because the manager is trading out of a single investment vehicle. There is no need to split tickets or enter into rebalancing trades; this leads to lower commissions. Some believe that there is also a benefit from the perspective of risk management: It is easier for a manager to watch one portfolio than two.

Yet while the master-feeder structure is the most common structure used by hedge fund managers for on- and offshore assets, some lawyers suggest that managers create and use the side-by-side structure. To do this, a manager operates one domestic fund structure and one offshore fund structure. The manager keeps the businesses completely separate, but allocates capital pari passu in accordance with asset flows. Many accountants believe that operating this way lets the manager manage for tax efficiency. However, it is considerably more work. Lawyers may try to dictate which structure you create and use. The key for you is to make sure that the vehicle you create makes sense for you from a cost and operational perspective.

When developing your offshore business model, you must keep in mind that regardless of your fund and management company's jurisdiction, as a U.S. citizen, you are subject to tax on your worldwide income. As a consequence, you cannot avoid paying tax on the fees that your fund generates. There are certain tax-deferral programs that you can use that will allow you to defer paying taxes on the income for a period of time. But eventually, unless the law is changed, you will have to pay the tax. Currently, the U.S. Congress is debating whether to abolish the tax-deferral programs that many hedge fund managers employ. However, an outcome on this issue is not expected for some time. The key for you is to make sure that you get counsel in regard to deferring taxes on fee income. The last thing you want to do is have a problem with the Internal Revenue Service over a simple issue. Remember, just because you are operating offshore, you and your investors are not out of the reach of the IRS. While specific tax and accounting issues are discussed in Chapter 4, remember for now that the IRS loves making examples out of hedge fund managers and other Wall Street executives who try to use various schemes to avoid paying taxes. Do the right thing and you won't have to worry. Don't give the IRS agents an excuse, because they are looking for these kinds of perpetrators to hold up to the light of day.

CHAPTER 4

Hedge Fund Accounting

Numbers never lie, and as we all know, numbers are critically important to the success of a hedge fund. Therefore, there is no more important task in the successful operation of a hedge fund than paying attention to the numbers.

As a manager, you need to pay attention to the amount of assets under management, the profits and losses, the number of investors, the operating costs, and the fees that you earn. Whether you like it or not, your job is to pay attention to the numbers at all times.

In the beginning, a lot of this work will be done by you and your team. However, along with the work that is done internally, you will also need to have work done externally. The people who provide these services are the accountant or auditor and the administrator.

This chapter is divided into two sections. The first section is on taxes and the audit functions of hedge fund operations; the second section is on the services provided by an administrator. Regardless of the assets under management, you will need to hire an auditor for the fund. If you operate an offshore fund, you will need an administrator. However, the jury is still out on whether you definitely need to have an administrator for an onshore fund. The current trend in the industry is that regardless of strategy, onshore funds are using administrators. This is directly related to a change in the makeup of investors that is discussed in Chapter 5.

As stated previously, when you decide to get into the hedge fund business, you will need to find a lawyer, a prime broker, an accountant, and an administrator (if you choose). The roles are pretty clear, and each will play an important function in the operation.

Your accountant will be involved in every aspect of the business from its inception, through ongoing maintenance, and right up until you wind down the fund some 20-odd years from now. The accountant you choose will be able to provide you with guidance on allocations of fees, capital and tax issues, and other financial nontrading issues that come up during the normal course of business. This person or organization will play an important role in keeping the numbers straight and giving you a clear picture of your financial status at all times.

As your business grows you will come to trust and value your relationship with your accountant over the life of your organization. That person or firm will become a trusted business adviser and friend, someone you come to rely on as your business grows.

During the start-up phase, as you are choosing an accountant or auditor (the names are synonymous), it is important to choose someone who has a good reputation in the hedge fund industry and who is respected by investors. Just as choosing a lawyer with a good reputation in the industry helps from a marketing standpoint, so does choosing an accountant. I would even posit that an accountant is more important than a lawyer. After all, the accountant is the one who keeps track of the numbers, and numbers are everything to investors.

Therefore, it is important to pick an accountant who not only has a good background in hedge funds, but one who has longevity and will be able to grow with you and your business. This accountant and his or her firm are going to have inside information on your operation. Therefore, you must feel a level of trust between your two firms. Remember, you will be opening up your robe for them to see the inner workings of your fund and the strategy you are using to make money. As a consequence, you want to make sure you like, trust, and respect each other.

Investors also need to be able to trust your accountants. After all, these accountants will be keeping track of their money in your fund. That is why choosing an accountant who has a good reputation in the hedge fund community is important. It is also important from a longevity standpoint, because if investors see you switching accountants, they may think that something is wrong with the way the fund is being managed or that the portfolio is ailing. This will be a red flag, and you want to avoid red flags! Switching accountants could adversely affect your ability to maintain and obtain investors.

In the beginning, the accountant will review your documents to ensure that the material specifies that the correct accounting methods and allocations are being used in the fund's operation. The accountant will also review the documents to make sure that any and all relevant tax issues have been addressed. It sounds simple and straightforward, but having lived through a number of fund start-ups, I can attest that this process can add gray hair to one's head. For the most part, all private placement memorandums cover the same things: strategies, risk, management, and so on. But for some reason, when it comes to accounting, there always seems to be a problem. The right thing to do is have the accountant review the documents before the material is finalized. This helps you avoid costly headaches in the future and definitely saves you from going prematurely gray.

Along with reviewing your documents, your initial conversations with the accountant will include discussing how partnership accounting works, how you will run your internal accounting efforts, and what you can expect from your prime broker and administrator to help make your business run smoothly.

PRICING

Your strategy will determine how securities in your portfolio are priced and marked. Obviously, securities that trade in the over-the-counter market or on an exchange are priced more easily than other types of investments that do not trade as frequently. In most cases, pricing is not an issue. However, there are situations in which hedge funds trade in esoteric or more-difficult-to-price securities, such as non-exchange-traded securities, mortgages, trade claims, and illiquid securities. These could pose a potential problem when it comes time to put a value on the portfolio. The pricing and valuation methods are easy to identify and use, and experienced accountants know the right and wrong way to price and put values on securities regardless of the liquidity. Most hedge fund accountants have significant experience in this area and are willing to work with you to make sure items are priced appropriately. The problem will arise when they come up with one price and you come up with another.

Unfortunately, there is no good rule of thumb in this area, except that you are always better off to err on the side of caution, regardless of how much money it may cost you. The worst thing that could happen to you as a new or existing manager is to have to restate performance results because something was priced incorrectly. Pricing should not be something that is a problem. If it does become a problem, it can and most likely will have significant ramifications for your business. This will not be worth it. There are many examples in which this specific issue has led to the demise of very large organizations.

Pricing illiquid securities became a hot button issue in 2005 and 2006. As a result, it is at the forefront of the sophisticated due diligence process. The following story illustrates my point.

My partner and I once looked at a fund that had nearly $800 million in assets under management, a strong management team, a solid infrastructure, and a very good track record. We liked the managers for their work in distressed securities, which include trade claims, accounts receivable, corporate bank loans, private insurance notes, and corporate bonds, and we were considering adding them to one of our portfolios. During the due diligence process, we spent a lot of time learning about how they operated their business and how they put the money to work. In one of our meetings, we spent a lot of time discussing the portfolio and especially their investments into trade claims. Trade claims are claims held by suppliers owed for goods or services by a company in bankruptcy. If an investor can buy the trade claim at the right price and can collect, investing in these can be extremely profitable.

The fund had made a significant amount of money investing in trade claims and had built expertise in research in this area of the distressed marketplace. The fund has truly become an expert in the distressed area. However, there is one small problem: How does one value a trade claim? It is nearly impossible to get a third party to come up with a valuation of a trade claim. For the most part, accountants are forced to take the word of the manager.

This was a problem for us and we chose not to invest because we could not get our hands around how they priced this specific area of their portfolio. Some very close friends of ours, people whom I have significant respect for in the hedge fund business, think this was a mistake on our part. Although we certainly did not believe that the manager was doing anything wrong, we were not comfortable enough with their process to pull the trigger and give them our money. Needless to say, the fund has done extremely well and has expanded its investments in this side of the distressed market.

Had the fund's accountant provided us with a level of comfort on this issue, we might have made a different decision. It all comes down to having enough information and being comfortable with the data.

You need to make sure that your investors are comfortable with the methodology used to price the portfolio and with any potential issues that may come up due to the new issue rules and side pockets. (Side pockets are discussed later in this section.) You do not want pricing to be a reason for an investor to decline your fund. That is why you should address it at the outset before the documents are completed. Doing so will avoid problems in the future.

Experienced accountants will not just help you ensure the documents are correct and the audit complete. They will also help with all financial aspects of your business and allow you to operate more efficiently. In addition, accountants will help you with issues that arise, such as when an investor withdraws his or her assets before you can divest from an illiquid investment. This is not new, but it is something that can be difficult to deal with.

One of the problems with trading or investing in illiquid securities is that occasionally a value can be realized only at the time of sale. This becomes an accounting problem if investors withdraw from the fund prior to your selling the position. Most funds deal with this issue through something called a *side-pocket account.* A side-pocket account allows the manager to segregate the specific investment from the rest of the portfolio and, based on an investor's capital, determine how much of it should be allocated to the capital account. Because the investment is "side-pocketed," its illiquidity and value do not have an effect on the overall performance of the fund. Profits or losses from the side-pocketed investment are allocated to existing and former investors and are not shared with new investors.

Over the past few years, hedge fund managers have discovered the value of investing in securities that are not publicly traded. Such securities offer significant growth potential, which means an opportunity to create positive returns. Unfortunately, valuation, accounting, allocation, distribution, and other difficulties associated with illiquid securities present unique issues for hedge fund managers. Unlike private equity and venture capital funds that are designed for these types of investments, hedge fund managers and their investors are not always equipped or ready for these types of investments. Therefore, hedge fund managers are using side pockets, also referred to as *designated investments,* to take advantage of these opportunities and segregate them from other aspects of the portfolio. By using a side pocket, you are able to achieve what you need—the simplicity of a hedge fund structure with the effective management of practical issues associated with investments in illiquid securities. By comparison, a private equity fund structure has capital calls, no redemptions, preferred returns, and clawbacks of the carried interest, among other things.

Side pockets are simple and flexible and thus have become a feature that most lawyers are adding to funds. Side pockets enable a fund manager to invest in securities that are or are becoming illiquid by allowing the fund manager to classify the securities as "designated" or "special" investments (i.e., held in a side pocket).

Once designated, the manager is able to use valuation, allocation, withdrawal, and distribution provisions specific to side pockets without affecting the general portfolio of the fund. Most documents being written today carry side-pocket provisions that typically permit a fund manager—if it is deemed to be in the best interest of the fund and its investors—to mark any investment as a designated investment, thus creating a side pocket. Investors are allocated an interest in a designated investment in proportion to their capital account. However, because these investments are difficult to value and trade, the manager treats this aspect of the portfolio as a private equity investment rather than as a hedge fund investment. This means that profits and losses are not distributed until the investment is monetized, and investors will not receive their interest in a designated investment immediately upon their withdrawal from the fund; they will have to wait until the fund exits the investment. As a fund manager, you are not entitled to receive an incentive allocation or performance fee attributable to the net gain of designated investments until the profits are realized. However, in some cases, you are able to charge your management fee. This will be spelled out in your documents and is something you should discuss with your lawyer and accountant if you believe that these types of investments will be part of the portfolio. In the end, managers use side pockets because they offer flexibility to go after illiquid investments and hold illiquid securities separate and apart from the general portfolio.

NASD RULES

Since March 2004, when the National Association of Securities Dealers (NASD), changed "the hot issue" rule to "the new issue" rule (Rule 2790), a lot of managers have been able to avoid using side pockets for some portfolio transactions that not all investors could take part in, not because the trades were in illiquid securities but because the rule did not allow certain individuals to participate in these types of transactions.

Prior to the rule change, *hot issues* were defined as any security that traded in the aftermarket at a premium to its initial public offering (IPO) price—basically any initial public offering. The NASD prohibited the allocation of gains or losses from these trades to restricted persons, including employees, officers, or associates of broker/dealers, senior bank officers, investment advisers, and people who worked at financial companies.[1]

Before the rule changes, most funds that traded in the initial public offering market had to side-pocket profit and losses from these trades and some investors were not able to reap the benefits from these transactions. The use of side pockets also forced funds and their auditors to do a lot of work to track and allocate these trades among the right investors during the audit and performance reporting process.

However, with the rule change, the use of side pockets has decreased significantly, and along with it, a number of accounting headaches that went with these trades and allocations. The new rule redefined a hot issue, changed its name to a *new issue,* and changed the definition of a restricted person. The rule now states that any new issue is defined as any IPO of an equity security. This means that regardless of whether it trades at a premium, it needs to be placed in a side pocket. The modification of the definition of a restricted person is extremely helpful and makes it easier for managers and accountants to track those who can and cannot participate in these trades.

The changes to Rule 2790 redefined *restricted person* as follows:

The definition of "restricted person" under the new rule includes NASD members, other broker/dealers and any officer, director, general partner, associated person, or employee of a member or other broker/dealer (other than a limited business broker/dealer—a broker/dealer that only engages in the purchase and sale of investment company/variable contract securities and direct participation program securities), any agent of a member or any other broker/ dealer (other than a limited business broker/dealer) that is engaged in the investment banking or securities business. It covers persons who own broker/dealers and are listed, or required to be listed, in Schedule A, Schedule B, and Schedule C of a Form BD (other than with respect to a limited business broker/dealer). Rule 2790 includes certain immediate family members of such specified persons.

In addition, the New Rule prohibits the sale of new issues to any senior officer of a bank, savings and loan institution, insurance company, investment company, investment advisory firm or any other institutional type account. The New Rule preserves the treatment of finders and fiduciaries of managing underwriters as restricted persons. However, in the case of a law firm or consulting firm, the restriction only applies to persons working on the particular offering.[2]

An additional change to the rule is something called the *de minimis exception*. As a hedge fund manager, you must pay attention to this. According to the de minimis exception, if your fund implements a procedure that ensures that a restricted person is not allocated more than 10 percent of the profit or loss from the trading of a new issue, then the fund does not have to side-pocket the trades—thereby avoiding extra accounting and administrative work on the portfolio.

As the manager, you need to make sure that you know who is and is not a restricted person and operate accordingly. In all subscription documents, the investor is asked questions specifically related to this issue. Your job is to track the information provided and share it with your service providers in order to make sure everything is done appropriately. Initially, this may seem like an overwhelming task; however, your administrator is there to help you with this. Your administrator is equipped to track this and other information to ensure that you comply with all rules and regulations applicable to customer information.

Once the documents are set and the business is launched, you will have little if any interaction with your accountant until it is time to go through an audit. Your monthly accounting functions will be done either internally by your chief financial officer or externally through an administrator. In either case, you will have limited interaction with your accountant until the audit begins.

THE AUDIT

The audit process is difficult and painful. It is the equivalent of going to the dentist and having your teeth pulled without Novocain or the use of the proper tools. You will need to collect significant amounts of data and material about your fund, your investors, your trades, your bank accounts, your standing with your lawyers and other service providers and provide all of this information to the accountant for review and audit. The most difficult aspect is that in most cases you have very little control over the flow of information. You will need to identify all of your service providers, including banks, brokers, the administrator, vendors, investors, and others and provide them with a request for information. Once the request is made, you have no control over how fast or how slow the service providers and investors respond. In some cases, the material can flow back to the accountant immediately; in others, it can be slow. Unfortunately for you, until all of the material is received, the audit cannot be completed, and this means that you can't issue the documents you need to send to investors and potential investors. In short, someone else is in control of your destiny. It is painful and it stinks.

An example of a hedge fund audit, as well as other pertinent financial documents, can be found at www.hedgeanswers.com.

As discussed previously, most hedge funds are set up as limited partnerships or limited liability companies. Yet for accounting purposes, they are treated as limited partnerships. This means that regardless of your structure, all funds are treated under limited partnership accounting rules. Unfortunately, partnership accounting is not easy and can be quite complex, regardless of strategy or assets under management. Each investor, or partner, is given a partner's capital account. This account tracks and values the partner or investor's interest in the fund throughout the entire life of the investment. The accountant provides a statement of account to the partner at year-end and, in some cases, when the fund has a break period. A *break period* is defined as anything that affects the partnership percentages (e.g., when a partner joins or leaves the fund). On the date of the break period, your accountant will tally all of the income and expenses, the portfolio holdings are marked to market, and in turn the partnership has a set valuation. The partnership agreement typically will determine when the break period will end—usually on the last day of a given month. The accountant will value the partnership on that date, and the new capital activity and percentages will become effective on the following day—usually the first of the month.[3]

TAX ISSUES

You will need to address a number of tax concerns during the year that take into consideration the difference between economic income and taxable income. Generally accepted accounting principles (GAAP) require the use of accrual-based accounting when determining economic income and taxable income, and the fund must comply with IRS regulations. Therefore, adjustments to economic income must be made prior to completing tax allocations. To do so, the accountant will review all of your financial records to determine your taxable loss or gain and then create the fund's tax return. In most cases, the accounting firm will complete the audit annually. This will provide you with a clear picture of the financial status of the fund, its performance and its stability. The audit can be a good tool for marketing purposes. Most investors will request an audited track record, and in having one at the ready, you will be able to move that much closer to getting more assets under management.

Over the next few pages, I have outlined a number of tax and audit issues that will affect your fund or your investors. The idea is to provide you with a brief understanding of issues that are important and give you an outline for discussion with your accountant and administrator. Hedge funds face many complex taxation issues. You would need to become a CPA to understand them all. The first thing to understand is that, because most U.S. hedge funds are organized as either limited partnerships or limited liability companies, they are subject to state general partnership laws. These state general partnership laws permit some form of limited partnership or limited liability company as structures that function as investment partnerships for the purposes of U.S. income tax.[4]

Following are some of the basic items that you should find helpful as you discuss accounting and audit functions with your accountant and administrator:

- Investment partnership classifications
- Allocation of earnings and realized gains and losses
- After-tax performance results

As the general partner, you have the flexibility to structure your compensation as either a fee or an allocation of income. This will be determined during the document creation stage of your business. Because it is considered more advantageous to the general partner and the investors, most general partners take their compensation as an allocation of net income and profits. This way, each underlying allocated item is not considered an expense of the partnership; rather, it retains its character in the hands of the general partner.[5]Allocations of income, expenses, gains, and losses to partners must meet the following criteria in order to ensure "substantial economic effect":

- They must be consistent with the underlying economic arrangements of the partners.
- They must have substance.
- They cannot be done merely to shift the tax consequences of transactions among the partners.[6]

Hedge funds classified as investment partnerships use either the *layering method* or the *aggregate method* to allocate realized profits or losses.

When the layering method is used, the fund allocates realized profits and losses to partners based on when the profits and losses occurred. The accountant takes into account each partner's respective portion of each security's unrealized gain or loss generated over time. This is individually recorded in an unrealized gain/loss account. When a particular security is sold, the resulting profit or loss is realized and is allocated to the investor's account.

In using the aggregate method, profits and losses realized are netted and allocated to partners. This differs from the layering method in that it does not specifically account for a partner's individual portion of the unrealized gain or loss for each security held by the fund. Rather, allocations are based on the unrealized appreciation or depreciation of the partnership's securities as a whole.[7] Most people agree that the aggregate method is easier to use than the layering method. Some experts believe that when used over time, the aggregate method generally provides for results that are not materially different from those produced using the layering method and that, therefore, because it is easier to use, it should be used! However, the accountants you choose will tell you which method they believe is best for your specific fund, and it is probably good to heed their advice.

Although in previous chapters I have discussed many of the differences between hedge funds and other investment vehicles, one thing that has not been discussed in depth is the fee structure that hedge funds imply. The popular press and many mutual fund companies like to say that hedge funds are expensive and that the products are overpriced—however, the fees are something that hedge fund investors have come to expect with this investment vehicle.

Most people consider the payment of an incentive fee to be a defining characteristic of the hedge fund industry. The fee structure is quite simple: A performance fee is charged that usually is equal to 20 percent of profits. A management fee is charged that is equal to 1 percent of assets under management. Over the years, managers have used things like high-water marks and hurdle rates to level the playing field between the manager and the investor.

Most hedge fund managers use the *high-water mark,* which simply states that the manager will receive his or her performance fee only when the value of the portfolio is greater than its previous greatest value. If the portfolio drops below its previous greatest value, then the manager must bring the portfolio back to its previous greatest value before again charging a performance fee. An example of a high-water mark is as follows: A million-dollar investment in a fund goes to $850,000 after one year. In this case, the manager would not be able to charge an incentive fee until he or she has brought the value of the investment back to its highest point, which in this case is $1 million.[8]

Hedge funds also use something called a *hurdle,* which is defined as the minimum return that the fund must achieve prior to the manager charging an incentive fee. In most cases, the hurdle rate is pegged to a relevant fixed-income benchmark; for example, the 10-year Treasury or LIBOR plus 100. Alternatively, the fund can use a fixed hurdle, such as 10 percent. If a fund has a hurdle rate of 10 percent but makes only 8 percent, the manager of the fund will not collect his or her incentive fee. However, if the fund earns 15 percent, the manager will earn the incentive fee on the spread between the return and the hurdle—in this instance, 5 percent.[9] Both of these tools are used to confirm to investors that the manager's interests are aligned with the investors' interests.

Calculating performance fees is a relatively easy exercise for an accountant when working with onshore funds. However, when a hedge fund is structured as a company that issues shares and publishes a net asset value (NAV)—this is what is done with most offshore funds—the means of calculating a performance fee becomes a bit more cumbersome. In this situation, a fund has several options for structuring its performance fee. According to Peter Testaverde of Goldstein Golub Kessler LLC, many managers of offshore funds choose to apply the performance fee at the fund level, which in some cases can cause an investor to be charged performance fees for performance that he or she did not achieve in the fund. In order to deal with this potential problem, many funds turn to something called the *method of equalization.* By using equalization, managers ensure that performance charged to individual investors correlates to the actual performance earned by the fund. When speaking to accountants, you will find that there are many different ways to accomplish equalization. According to one discussion paper, the most common are the following:

- Equalization shares approach (also called the share-series or multiseries approach)
- Equalization/depreciation deposit approach
- Equalization adjustment approach[10]

Most hedge funds use the equalization shares approach, which requires that the fund issue a separate series of shares with each opening. Each series is tracked individually, which results in the ability to calculate the appropriate performance fee for each of the series. Most believe that this is a straightforward method of equalization. It does, however, become somewhat confusing to investors who make multiple investments in a fund, which results in multiple NAVs. The year-end change in a shareholder's outstanding share balances and ensuing NAVs also sometimes adds to this confusion.[11]

To learn more about the other equalization methods and how they are used, it is best to consult with your accountant or administrator. Equalization is a very complicated calculation, regardless of the approach, and requires sophisticated record-keeping capabilities. Most administrators and accountants are capable of handling this for you—but be careful in determining which method you use, because it will affect your ability to raise money.

ADMINISTRATORS

Today, in light of the increasing calls for regulation and the purported increase in due diligence efforts, many investors are demanding to see an audited track record and audited financials before they will invest with a fund. The audit performed by your accountant will be used for this purpose. And while the audit is done once a year, many onshore funds have started using fund administrators to track their performance and asset inflows and outflows. Prior to the calls for more due diligence and third-party verification, many onshore funds performed the day-to-day fund accounting functions themselves using data provided by their banks and prime brokers. However, as investors have demanded more and more information, including information verified by third parties (objective sources), firms have begun to use administrators to provide these services and functions to their organizations. There is an increase in cost for using an administrator. However, in most cases the use of these service providers does help in the marketing process. Consequently, the benefits outweigh the costs.

Hedge funds use an administrator to provide the following services on a monthly basis: bookkeeping, independent portfolio pricing and valuation, and the tracking of asset inflows and outflows. The administrator will also help the fund keep track of the management and incentive fee earned by the manager.

Think of an administrator as your external accounting department. The administrator will keep a general ledger, maintain all books and records, be an objective source for portfolio pricing, and verify your track record. The service provider will also help with compliance services including anti-money laundering needs, as required by the USA Patriot Act.

An administrator will service your investors and provide the administrative and operational services that are often both difficult and time-consuming for a manager to do, regardless of the size of the organization. Your administrator will also provide you with financial, tax, and compliance reporting—functions that are going to make your firm run more smoothly and efficiently.

Some fund managers believe that they can provide the administration services themselves. However, those who do often become overwhelmed by the amount of work that is needed to ensure that things are done properly. Additionally, in the beginning it can be quite expensive to hire in-house accountants and a chief financial officer, the people with the necessary skills and experience to complete the administration of the fund in an efficient and timely manner.

By contracting a third party, you are hiring an expert to provide necessary staff, infrastructure, and supervision of the work performed. The administrator's only job will be to provide correct and timely performance of duties and to make sure that your operation complies with all applicable rules, regulations, and laws. In doing so, you will be able to take advantage of the scale of the administrator's operation and experience and, most likely, will be able to achieve the same ends in a cheaper and more efficient manner than if you performed all administrator responsibilities in-house.

Hedge fund administrators provide you with client servicing, administration, and accounting for your fund, typically billed on an asset-based fee basis subject to monthly minimums. There are a number of different types or kinds of administrators offering services to the hedge fund community. The biggest difference is that some administrators provide a "light NAV" service while others provide "full NAV" service. The difference is in the number of tasks the company will perform for you. Most of the larger administrators offer only full NAV services because of potential liability issues.

In most cases, you will have some responsibility for client servicing, administration, and accounting, but the bulk of the work will be done by the service provider. One area where administrators can be extremely helpful is in compliance with the rules, regulations, and laws, especially regarding anti–money laundering and know-your-client laws. It is here where they add significant value and where you will be thankful that they are involved in your operation. They can also help out with new rules regarding registration.

There are many reasons for using an administrator. Some believe that by outsourcing administration functions, a manager can greatly reduce expenses and overhead for a fund and its investment adviser, because it eliminates the need for a larger administrative and operational staff. Using a third party also allows you to take advantage of skills, talents, and systems that you may find too expensive to purchase through your investment adviser. In most cases, an administrator will give you access to people trained, and often certified, in accounting, finance, and operations who have significant experience and expertise that you could not afford to hire that you would not want to carry as overhead in your operation.

While cost savings will be a direct benefit of using an administrator, the real advantage will come from the investors. Existing and potential investors will really appreciate that you use an independent third party to verify your funds' operating results. And marketing, my friend, is the main reason to use an administrator.

Over the past few years, one of the press's main topics about hedge funds has been the lack of information provided to investors. The media seems to be constantly questioning the size, shape, and performance of the industry and is often critical of the lack of standardized reporting requirements. One method for dealing with this issue is to provide investors with information that is verified by a third party. This can help overcome certain objections raised by investors during the due diligence process.

Nothing forces you, as an onshore fund operator, to use a hedge fund administrator. However, offshore fund managers do not have a choice in the matter. Since fund managers cannot operate offshore funds, they are simply employed to manage the fund through a subadvisory agreement.

The offshore fund will have an independent board of directors that will dictate how the fund is operated and who is managing it. And, just as mutual fund investors could potentially fire Fidelity as the manager of Magellan, offshore investors can potentially fire the manager of the hedge fund. This is something that many managers find difficult to understand and hard to believe.

To get a clear understanding, the best thing to do is to consult your firm's counsel. While you could be fired as the manager of the offshore fund that you launched and paid for, the reality is that it most likely will never happen. There is too much riding on the hedge fund industry for this to happen. Nevertheless, because of this real but far-fetched possibility, the role of an offshore administrator is much more important to the continued success of the operation and is not something a fund can be without.

As I discussed in Chapter 3, offshore hedge funds are typically organized as corporations in countries such as the Cayman Islands, British Virgin Islands, and Bermuda. Investors in these products include non-U.S. residents and U.S. tax-exempt entities (e.g., pension funds, charitable trusts, foundations, and endowments). Due to UBTI issues, U.S. tax-exempt investors use offshore hedge funds because they may be subject to taxation if they invest in domestic hedge funds.

Offshore funds use administrators to perform many of the same functions that onshore administrators provide, including pricing the portfolio, calculating the fund's net asset value, maintaining fund records, processing investor transactions, and handling fund accounting. The sponsor of an offshore hedge fund—the manager—appoints a board of directors to provide oversight activities for the fund. These boards, while appointed by the manager/sponsor, operate independently of the investment adviser and have the ultimate authority over who manages the fund and its assets. The board works closely with the administrator to ensure that everything is being done in the fund according to the offering documents.

THE TEN COMMANDMENTS

The role of offshore fund administration changed dramatically in 1997 when the Clinton administration enacted its tax-relief program, which repealed items that most people in the investment world called the Ten Commandments. First enacted by the Foreign Investors Tax Act of 1966 (FITA), these regulations outlined 10 activities that limited the access of foreign investment in U.S. securities. The Ten Commandments required that any U.S.-managed fund have 10 functions performed at its offices outside the United States for the fund to be exempt from certain U.S. taxes on its U.S.-source income. These 10 functions were as follows: (1) communicating with shareholders; (2) communicating with the general public; (3) soliciting sales of the company's stock; (4) accepting subscriptions of new shareholders; (5) maintaining the principal corporate records and books; (6) auditing the company's accounts; (7) disbursing payments of dividends, legal fees, accounting fees, and directors' fees; (8) publishing or furnishing the offering and redemption price of the company's shares; (9) conducting shareholders' and directors' meetings; and (10) making redemptions of the company's stock.[12]

In the wake of the repeal, managers no longer need to work with an offshore company, but can potentially use any of the onshore administrators to handle this aspect of their business.

Now, legislation enacted more than nine years ago allows you, as a fund manager, to potentially get a better price for the services that you need to administer your fund. The repeal of the Ten Commandments has caused the marketplace to grow significantly by allowing new firms to change the competitive environment. This has resulted in a positive impact for hedge fund managers and investors on fees and service quality. Recently, since late 2004, competitive pressures have also led to a consolidation among many in the fund administration industry, resulting in fewer players offering more services. However, most believe that this consolidation has not negatively impacted price or the overall quality of service.

When it comes to selecting an administrator, you need to have a clear understanding of the services you are in need of, what you want, and what you expect to receive from the service provider. To make this decision, you must go through a due diligence process on the service provider, and due diligence means more than just getting a quote for the business.

The landscape is littered with hedge fund administrators. Even with the recent consolidation, there are still a significant number of firms, both large and small, that offer administration services to both the onshore and offshore community. A good starting place for names and contact information is the appendix of this book. However, you can also search on the Web through sites such as www.hedgeworld.com and www.albournevillage.com.

During the due diligence process, you will be able to immediately weed out firms that are just not right for you and your firm. The reasons will be obvious: price, service quality, and reputation will allow you to weed out those that are not worth talking to and should be bypassed from the start. One way to get started is to develop a questionnaire that you submit to firms you are interested in to gather data on their operations. Ask your lawyer and accountant for ideas when crafting the questionnaire. You might also be able to find a prepackaged questionnaire on the Web. However, most of these forms are not free, and you may need to join an organization to get them.

ADMINISTRATOR DUE DILIGENCE

I suggest that you write your own questionnaire. Make sure you ask how net asset values are calculated, where the firm gets its pricing, and what sort of business continuity programs are in place in the event of a disaster. When you and your team are reviewing the responses, you must feel that you have a good understanding of the size and scope of the firm's business. More important, you must understand how you will fit into the organization. Likewise, keep in mind that just because you have received information on a company does not mean you are ready to make a decision. You need to use the material to get a good understanding of the organization, meet with the team that will be working on your fund, and talk to clients. Regarding the last point, I am not a firm believer in references, because rarely does anyone offer as a reference someone whose perspective and potential statements are not a foregone conclusion. Therefore, you need to do a lot of work, get a feel for the firm, and understand the level of respect it commands in the industry before you make your final decision.

One thing you should do is talk to clients of the firm using it for the same services you are looking to contract. For example, if you are trading long/short equity, you don't necessarily need to talk to a fixed-income arbitrage fund manager. Your prime broker should also be able to help you during this process. Most have a good feel for what is happening on the Street and will give you good, honest feedback about the people you are considering to service your fund.

As a money manager, you need to approach your choice of administrator the same way you would pick a stock or a bond. You need to obtain some market intelligence to determine whether the person can actually add some value your organization. I recommend you do the following during the due diligence process:

- Do a site visit. Check out the firm's offices—particularly the office that is going to do your work.
- Talk to the people who will be working on your fund—you need to get past the sales force.
- Make sure that your technology and systems will plug into theirs, and vice versa.
- Make sure they have other clients who invest in the same instruments as you and that you will not be a guinea pig for a new pricing system or service.
- Make sure you get the feeling that you matter.
- Make sure they understand exactly what you are trading and have a comfort level for pricing the securities, regardless of how exotic the portfolio might be.
- Have your counsel review the administrator's standard agreement and get a detailed procedure manual—a term sheet, if you like—to explain exactly what the administrator is going to do and who is responsible, in which office, for each specific task.[13]

There are more items that need to be checked. However, the preceding list will give you a good handle on the operation and the firm's ability to deliver. A few other things that will help you in the decision process include the following:

- Does the administrator have an independent electronic price feed? This is important, because you don't want them to rely on you or your broker for pricing.
- What sort of technology are they using and how up-to-date are their systems?

The idea is that you need to complete a thorough and meaningful due diligence exercise on the administrator before the firm is hired. When the selection process is complete, it is important to remember that just because something costs more does not mean it is better, and just because something is cheap does not mean it is bad. You need to pick the firm that you and your team feel most comfortable with and that you believe will deliver exactly what you need.

A good administrator should add value to a fund and its operation. Unfortunately, even with significant advancements in technology, fund administration is still a very labor-intensive business: The services will not be cheap. In the end, you need to make sure that your administrator delivers. Only by doing much due diligence will you ensure that you have found the right firm.

CHAPTER 5

ERISA, UBTI, and Offshore Funds

At cocktail parties, you will introduce yourself as a hedge fund manager. From here to eternity, you will do the same at pretty much any social event. It will become your moniker and your persona. It is your identity, and you will like it, be proud of it, and wear it on your sleeve.

A hedge fund manager is what you have become, and you will tell people with pride and vigor. You will be happy as long as you raise a lot of money and your fund performs well. If your fund raises no money and its performance is lousy, then you will be telling people you are looking for a job.

It is quite an accomplishment to go out on your own, and you should be proud. Remember, however, that humility is also a good thing. When push comes to shove, you are no different than any other entrepreneur. Be it the guy who owns the shoe store or the gal who owns the dry cleaner, you all have something in common—the survival of your business.

As I stated in previous chapters, most hedge funds fail because of their inability to gather assets. They are unable to survive because they simply can't get people to invest in their products. Even though most managers know what to do with the money once they get it, they don't know how to go out and get it.

In Chapter 9, you will read about funds that have succeeded and funds that have failed. Your job is to learn from both the negatives and positives and make something good happen for you and your partners. Before we get to that good stuff, I must say that it has been my experience that people always like reading case studies. But first, we need to examine a number of issues that surround raising the capital. Specifically, you need to learn about ERISA, UBTI, and offshore funds.

Once the work is finished and your business becomes operational, you will move into what I call the *business sustainability phase* of your operation. You enter this phase exactly at the point when you realize that you no longer need to inject money to cover your operating costs and that your firm is self-sufficient. This is a big day for most entrepreneurs and one that should be cherished and enjoyed.

When you hit this critical mass, you will then be able to focus all of your attention on growing and building the business and maintaining your ability to sustain the operation. Most hedge fund managers believe that the key for survival over the long term is to control as many assets as they can and make sure that those assets are sticky. I believe this to be completely true and that it is the mantra we all should live by. Remember that *sticky* means that regardless of performance, the assets will stay with you for the long haul. These are not assets that come from your friends, family, or colleagues. I am talking about assets that come from institutions with a well-defined and succinct mandate to invest in hedge funds, organizations that believe in and subscribe to your ability to manage money over long periods of time.

Unfortunately for most, gaining access to these assets is extremely hard. Most people are not willing to put in the time, build the relationships, and do the dance with the powers that be to enable them to receive an allocation from these investors. Instead, they move away from this area of the marketplace and focus on the easy marks. This is a mistake. You need to construct and implement a plan to go after large pools of assets that you can control or maintain in your fund for a long time. Assets that fit this bill are those put to work by pensions, endowments, and other institutional investors. I must emphasize that they are not assets that come from funds of funds.

In today's competitive environment, most investors chase returns. They look for the hot manager and dive in exactly when they should be running for the hills. You need to go after the smart money—the organizations that make good, well-thought-out investment decisions based on a manager's expectation for long-term performance.

For as long as there have been hedge funds, smart money, endowments, and institutions have been investing in these types of products. These people are smart, good at what they do, and understand the value of going long and short the market. More recently, pension plans and other retirement programs have started to invest in hedge funds as a direct result of their inability to capture performance from long-only investment products. The people who run these programs understand that they need something new to help them meet their needs during low- or no-growth periods. As a result, they have started to invest significantly in hedge funds. Some organizations have been investing in these products for quite some time, and these people are well-covered by the industry. Other state and local organizations have just started their foray into the land of hedge funds and are looking for a manager to help them with returns.

As a manager, you need to consider how to go after these pools of assets and gain access to this capital. To do so, you need to understand the rules and regulations surrounding the plans investing in hedge funds.

Since the spring of 2000, I have been running programs on hedge funds for the New York Society of Securities Analysts. The programs range in length from one 8-hour, single-day session to four 2-hour sessions. They consist of interviews and information about everything that is hedge fund–related. Generally, I cover the evolution, current status, and future of the industry. I also talk about structures, styles, and strategies. Both programs consist of real-life people from the hedge fund industry who come in and talk about their specific areas of the business. Much like Bravo's popular series *Inside the Actor's Studio*, mine is called Understanding Hedge Funds.

Over the years, the syllabus has changed considerably as new topics and issues arise. However, two things remain constant: the sections on structures and tax issues. In February 2006, I held the winter program. It was a good day. Turnout was strong and the feedback generally positive. However, there were two major complaints: (1) People wanted to see more hedge fund managers as speakers, and (2) there was too much information on taxes and regulation. I agree with the former and disagree with the latter. As I discussed in Chapter 4, auditors and accountants are people who will make important contributions to your business. As far as I am concerned, I think that you can never know too much about tax issues and regulations and how they impact your business. This chapter is about specific tax issues and regulations that you need to pay strict attention to as you build your onshore and offshore fund and as you prospect for assets.

ERISA

In 1974, Congress passed the Employee Retirement Income Security Act, or ERISA, with the intention to set up uniform federal standards to protect private employee pension plans from fraud and mismanagement. The legislation regulates the financing, vesting, and administration of pension plans for workers in private business and industry. Basically, it ensures that employees' plans will be there for them when they retire. ERISA is huge in the investment community. Most managers love to get ERISA money, but they hate the tasks and potential headaches that go along with having the assets in their portfolios. However, what saves most managers is that most of the responsibility is placed on those who make the investment decision to invest in a specific fund or pool. As long as they (in this case the fund managers) manage the money based on their assignment, they are protected if something goes wrong. Yet in today's litigious society, lawyers will sue everyone and everything involved with a transaction should a fund blow up or post significant losses. Yet as long as managers stick to their investment guidelines, they will generally not be held accountable for their mistakes. However, if they invest in illiquid securities when they were told to invest only in liquid securities, or if they trade futures when not authorized to do so, then they will have a problem. Needless to say, there can and will be headaches associated with these assets.

There are two problems with going after these types of assets. First, there are significant rules and regulations that accompany the acceptance of these monies that, if violated, can cause you significant problems. Second, you need to make sure that the allocators of these monies deem you and your fund worthy of the assets.

As the new kid on the block, you are going to have to figure out a way to navigate this area of the investment world. In my opinion, you should do it only in the company of the people who work with you or for you. You do not need to hire an outside consultant to help you with this work. Most people who hold themselves out as experts in raising assets from pension plans and endowments are worth little more than the paper the contract is written on. There are very few successful third-party marketers, and it would be a shame for you to hire one believing that such a person will help you raise assets only to then realize that he or she does nothing but waste your time and ability to gain access to this area of the marketplace.

I believe that you should go after a group of these investors and target them yourself. Getting the data points on their assets, their investments, and the contact information is relatively easy and inexpensive. It might take longer than you like and may be extremely frustrating, but in the end it will be worth it because you will understand the process firsthand and you will own the assets.

Unquestionably, some consider ERISA assets to be the most lucrative and most difficult assets to attain and manage. These pools are extremely large and very sticky, but they are often run by individuals, committees, and consultants who take a long time to make a decision to actually deliver assets into a fund.

There is a lot of responsibility placed on the manager of ERISA money. First and foremost, there is the 25 percent rule, which states that a fund will not accept more than 25 percent of its assets from ERISA plans. ERISA plans are defined as retirement accounts, such as pension, Keogh, and other plans that provide for people in their golden years. By limiting your ERISA assets to under 25 percent, you are not required to do anything differently, nor do you accept any additional responsibility for the assets, except to ensure that you never have more than 25 percent of your assets from these types of investors. The calculation is quite simple. If you have $100 in total assets under management and $26 comes from ERISA plans, then you are over the limit and in trouble. If you have $24, you are fine. It is mission critical to keep an eye on the asset level and the percentage. The last thing you want to deal with is going over the limit and the headaches that come from this sort of mistake.

However, if you do go over the 25 percent limit, your fund will then be considered "a plan," and this distinction creates enormous responsibility.

As long as you do not violate the 25 percent rule, you are free to operate no differently than you would with any other assets you manage. You should treat the investors exactly the same and just pay attention to the asset barrier.

In summer of 2006, Congress passed and President Bush signed the Pension Protection Act of 2006 which changed how investment managers calculate the 25 percent test to determine if the fund holds plan assets. Under the new law, governmental plans, foreign plans, and certain religious plans no longer count in the test. Also, under the old rule, if a fund that is considered to have plan assets invests in an entity, only the portion of assets of the investments that is attributed to plan investors counts in the test. The new rule makes it much easier for funds to meet the 25 percent test because a number of large investors are no longer counted.

By not accepting more than 25 percent of your assets from ERISA plans, which means that you forgo the extra responsibility that goes along with becoming a plan, the responsibility for the investment rests with the people who made the investment in your fund. The burden, if you will, of making sure the investment lives up to expectations is then placed on those who are fiduciaries for the plan. The plan sponsor, plan director, and consultant, along with anyone else who shares in asset allocation duties, also share in the liabilities of the assets that are placed with you. This means that the due diligence process will most likely be quite detailed and intense.

During the due diligence process, the plan allocators need to look at a number of different factors and pieces of information to ensure that they are making the right investment decisions. One of the first things they will look at is the prudence of the investment. Allocators or fiduciaries must give appropriate consideration to the facts and circumstances that are relevant to the particular investment in your fund. This means that they need to think about why they are making this investment, how they are making this investment, whether it make sense for the plan, and whether the plan warrants these types of investments. They will question whether it is too risky or not risky enough, whether it does what it is supposed to do, and whether the managers meet the due diligence requirements.

To make these types of decisions, fiduciaries need to also look at the composition of portfolios, the positions in your fund, and any relation to any other fund in which they invest. Diversification is very important. They do not want to have all of their eggs in one basket. They need to look at things like liquidity and transparency, projected returns, where the returns will fall based on prior performance, and other market indices. They need to look at all of the things that make sense for making an investment in your fund. During the due diligence process, the fiduciaries and their agents are constantly asking the same questions over and over again in an attempt to uncover information about your fund. They need to be able to answer this question: Does an investment in the fund make sense for their plan?

Over the past few years, in direct correlation to the bursting of the technology bubble, diversification has emerged as one of the biggest issues during the due diligence process. Fiduciaries want to ensure that there is enough diversification in their pools of investments to minimize the risk of large losses, not only with your fund but with yours in relation to all of their other investments.

Their job is to consider a number of different issues in order to make the most appropriate and sound investment decision for their plan. One thing that plan investors are looking to do is to ensure that they have geographic dispersion of the investments.

For example, prior to 1998, many plans were investing in emerging-market funds. These funds had, for the most part, a high concentration of assets in the debt of the former Soviet Union and other nations around the world. When the Russian debt crisis struck, many funds, specifically in the emerging-market areas, were wiped out. Those funds, along with a number of global macro funds, saw their portfolios plunge to zero. This hurt investors of all shapes and sizes. In particular, it hurt investors who did not have the foresight to see that a global debt crisis could occur and wreak havoc on their investment portfolios.

While geographic dispersion of investments is a key factor in the investment decision process, investors are also thinking about the dispersion of investments and distribution among industries. This becomes very important if you are operating a sector fund. From a plan perspective, allocators who are doing due diligence on your fund may want to know portfolio positions. Why? Because they are going to want to ensure that all of the risks associated with an investment in your fund are understood. If you say that you are a technology fund, then it is understandable that you are going to have greater or more concentrated risks than a long/short fund that specializes in growth stocks.

The key for you is to know that they are expecting you to provide them with the most accurate and meaningful information. The last thing you want to have happen is for a plan to have to redeem because allocators have too many concentrated positions and are worried about the risks associated with the investment in your fund relative to others in their portfolio.

Plans also look for position-level transparency. For example, they may want to ensure that they do not have too much overlap between an investment in a technology fund and an investment in a large-cap fund. The plan wants to make sure that both are not overweighted in Google or Microsoft.

The plans should not be allowed to have too much concentration in one specific sector of the market or one specific company because of the fear that if the trade goes away from them, they could have potentially significant losses and not be able to meet their obligations to their members.

During the due diligence process, you need to make sure that you ask lots of questions so you fully understand the needs, expectations, and requirements of their investment portfolios. Since the bubble burst in the early part of this century, and because the stock market has not met performance expectations, many ERISA plans are finding themselves underfunded and at risk of not meeting impending liabilities. In some cases, the people making investment decisions are relaxing requirements; in other cases, they are making them more stringent. It all comes to down to what kind of shape the plan is in and how economic and market conditions are affecting its ability to meet its liabilities.

Investors need to look underneath the investments. They need to dig down into the portfolio, to look at how your fund is structured and how your fund is invested. As the manager, you must do what is required during the due diligence process. Once you deliver what they need, they will deliver what you need—sticky money.

As a manager, you have some rights as well, and you can demand information from the potential investors. I suggest that you get as much information as possible about the plan, its directors, consultants, investments, needs, and expectations. During due diligence, investors are going to ask you all sorts of questions. While you need to provide them with answers, you also need to ask them lots of questions as well. This is a two-way street and a partnership. They are providing you with capital, and you are providing them with returns to meet their obligations. Make sure you review the plan documents, because you need to make sure that any investment they make with you is made in accordance with the plan's document.

You cannot just accept the assets from the plan and then invest. You need to do your homework. The right move is to understand that the plan is going to make an investment. You need to learn what they are going to do and determine what you are going to do for them. It is important to conduct this exercise and confirm with your lawyer that everything is being done appropriately.

Now, as I stated, the interesting thing about these types of investments is that the fiduciaries are personally liable for plan losses resulting from any breach of fiduciary duties. This means that if they act inappropriately, they are going to have to make up their losses if the fund loses money. The fiduciary may also be liable for the difference between the actual earnings and the hypothetical return. As an example, if a fund benchmarks itself against the S&P 500, and that index is up 30 percent but the investments are up only 20 percent, then the plan could come after the fiduciary and make that person pay up.

However, before that plan can come after a fund, a real loss has to be incurred. The loss cannot just be hypothetical; it must be real. Obviously, a fiduciary may be removed for a breach in fiduciary duty, even if no loss is incurred by the plan. Nonetheless, a fiduciary is subject to the 20 percent penalty, or even jail time, for knowingly participating in a breach of fiduciary duty.

These plans are going to bring specific issues to you, and you need to be cognizant of them. Before you get started, you need to answer one question: Who is the fiduciary? The fiduciary is a person who exercises discretionary control with respect to management of such a plan. He or she exercises control regarding the management and disposition of assets. And the fiduciary renders investment advice for a fee and other compensation. This is where many people sometimes get in trouble. First of all, some fiduciaries act on behalf of a plan and a fund, yet they do not disclose the fact that they or one of their affiliates is generating fee income from their work. There have been situations in which fund managers are compensating these people for bringing them assets. They often do not disclose this to the plans that they are working for. In turn, they are paid on both sides of the transaction.

Over the past few years, this has been a very big issue and something that most plans are paying attention to. Major newspapers have published several articles on this, especially focusing on the fact that a number of large consulting groups have gotten into trouble for entering into deals in which they are paid a fee for bringing in assets to a fund, even though they are supposed to be providing objective advice to that fund.

As a manager, it is best to avoid these conflicts. In the end, no matter how much money comes your way through this type of arrangement, it is not going to be worth it.

Understanding the issues surrounding ERISA investments is critical to the success of your business. It is also important that you fully understand unrelated business taxable income (UBTI). Although I briefly discussed UBTI in Chapter 4, the following pages provide insight and information on the subject in much greater detail.

In the class I teach on hedge funds, we spend nearly a whole day talking about UBTI issues. Understanding the concept and regulations will make you a better a manager and help you reach a thorough understanding of the need for offshore funds.

UBTI came about not long after the adoption of the income tax in 1913. At that time, the government challenged the right of charitable organizations to use their exemptions to shield business profits from taxation. The government challenged the exempt status of a charitable organization that operated a business bearing no relation to its expressed charitable purpose.

The government, in enacting the new law, reasoned that if, for example, a church opened up a Burger King across the street from a McDonald's owned by the McDonald's Corporation, all of the proceeds from the Burger King should not be considered tax-exempt merely because it was owned by a tax-exempt charity, such as a 501(c)(3) tax-exempt organization—in this case the church. Because all of the profits from the McDonald's would be taxable (i.e., the company that owned the restaurant was a taxable entity), the church that owned the Burger King had an upper hand: It didn't matter whether the burgers tasted better or whose fries the market preferred. Since the Burger King would not have to pay taxes, it can compete unfairly against McDonald's because its overall expenses and costs of doing business are lower.

It was assumed that the organization that was operating in a tax-exempt environment had a leg up on the organization that was operating in a taxable one. Therefore, the government argued that if the church is running a business that is not part of, equal to, similar to, or considered to be part of its day-to-day operations, it should pay tax on the revenue derived from that operation.

Consequently, the government successfully challenged the exempt status of the charitable organization that was operating businesses that bore no relationship to its organization, and the charity in question lost its tax-exempt status in relation to those businesses. However, the government was unsuccessful in its challenge when the organization in question used its business profits for the exempt purpose. For example, it probably would not have been successful if the Burger King also had a church in it or if it had some relation to the day-to-day activities of the church.

The idea behind the government's challenge was twofold: (1) It was believed that it allowed people to compete unfairly, and (2) the government lost revenue from these operations. In the end, the government was able to impose a tax on business activities that were not substantially related to the exercise or performance of the organization's purpose or function.

This meant that the church could still get into the hamburger business. However, it would then have to pay tax on the business and its profits.

Even with the ruling and regulation, certain items of income were specifically excluded from taxation and deemed not to be unfair competition. The government specifically said that dividends, interests, royalties, and rents from property were acceptable. However, it stated that dividend interest payments with respect to securities, royalties, and rents other than rent dependent on the net profits derived from the use of the property were to be specifically excluded from unrelated business taxable income.

Certain items of income were specifically excluded from taxation. These included dividends, interest royalties, and rents from real property. The law also included a provision that resulted in the taxation of a portion of rental income from real estate of indebtedness that was incurred to acquire or improve real estate debt-financed real estate.[1] The Tax Reform Act of 1969 stated that all exempt organizations would be subject to UBTI and, furthermore, that the tax would be imposed on virtually any type of debt-financed property. The tax is computed on unrelated business income tax on the exempt organization. This is not generally the net business income of the exempt organization. This income can result directly from the activities of an investment partnership engaged in nonsecuritized transactions (i.e., active management of trade claims or distressed debt, or indirectly from investment in other entities). Exempt organizations must make estimated tax payments. Underpayments are subject to estimated tax penalties. Compliance is virtually impossible. A Form 220 is used to compute the estimated tax penalty for exempt organizations subject to the corporate or trust rates. The prior year's tax exemption can be used to avoid estimated tax penalties.[2]

According to Maury Cartine, executive vice president at BISYS Alternative Investment Services, the problem with debt-financed property is that it needs to be defined. Is it property acquired or carried with debt? Prior to the expansion of the debt-finance property rules, debt financing was frequently used in bootstrap transactions. For example, a charity would acquire stock on an installment basis from a seller. The seller would receive long-term capital gains treatment on the collections of the installment note. A charitable organization would liquidate the corporation and lease the business assets to the new corporation operated by the seller. Then the rental income would be exempt and the charitable organization would use the rent to pay the installment note. The seller would maintain control of the business, and the charitable organization would keep the rent from the installment note. "This was a problem because the government would lose the tax associated with this transaction," he said. "The expansion of the debt finance property rules did away with these types of situations."

In the world of hedge funds, the UBTI issue arises as a result of leverage in portfolios and the financing of funds with lines of credit. Initially, it was believed that exempt organizations should be able to invest idle assets to support exempt activities. However, the government questioned the use of the funds and margin and its relation to the exempt organization's activities. The government says that exempt organizations that invest in onshore (i.e., taxable) entities are no longer exempt and are now forced to pay tax on their earnings. As a result, most of these investors have taken their investments offshore to mitigate the impact of UBTI. The key for these investors is to avoid these issues by putting their assets in investments in offshore funds. If you do not want to deal with UBTI issues and do not want your tax-exempt clients to have to deal with UBTI issues, do not give them access to your onshore fund. Tax-exempt investors who invest in onshore funds will be burdened with significant tax consequences as a result of the investment. These issues can be totally avoided by moving the money offshore.

Several recent rulings affecting UBTI are significant to you as a hedge fund manager. The first is the short-sale ruling. The government says that gains on short sales that are not debt-financed income do not result in unrelated business income tax. The ruling does not specifically address losses on short sales, but most accountants believe that losses should be excluded from the complication of unrelated business income tax.

Another issue of interest is the ruling surrounding the sale of partnership interests. If a partnership interest is sold in a partnership that owned debt-financed property, the gain of the sale is subject to unrelated business income tax. This rationale should extend to losses and exemptions of limited partnership interests.

When it comes to commodities and futures contracts, gains from these transactions are not considered debt-financed income, even though current cash deposits are required by the Commodities Futures Trading Commission. Losses should be treated the same way.[3]

To avoid all of these issues, you need to have an offshore fund that is open to U.S.-tax-exempt investors. The advantage of offshore funds is that there are no unrelated business income taxes whatsoever. Consequently, tax-exempt organizations do not risk running afoul of their exemption. Also, there is no look-through provision for debt-financing companies under the control of offshore corporations. To learn more about the effects of UBTI on your business and your investors, you should talk to your accountant. He or she will be able to provide you with greater detail on how UBTI comes into play for your specific fund and organization.

OFFSHORE FUNDS

When you launch your business, you probably will not be thinking about onshore and offshore investors. You will just be thinking about investors. However, the last few pages should have made it abundantly clear why there is a need for an offshore structure.

You are probably right in initially not wanting to think about offshore structures. However, you must ensure that you have a product that is right for your market. In most cases, setting up an onshore and an offshore structure is the right way to go, even though it can add significantly to the cost of the operation. The key is to determine where your assets will be coming from and then to ensure that you have a home for them when they arrive.

An offshore fund provides a number of tax benefits that are attractive to both nontaxable U.S. investors and U.S. domestic managers. The first is the opportunity for foreign investors to invest without running the risk of owing U.S. taxes on their investments. In light of the repeal of the Ten Commandments, a foreign corporation—which is what the offshore hedge fund is—that trades securities for its own account is deemed not to be engaged in a trade or business within the United States, even if the principal office of the foreign corporation is located within the United States. This means that it and its investors are not subject to any tax liability.

Using an offshore vehicle, offshore investors or nontaxable U.S. investors avoid effectively connected income and capital gains. In an offshore fund, foreign partners of domestic partnerships trading securities for their own accounts are deemed not to be engaged in trade or business within the United States. Therefore, the foreign partner's share of partnership income will no longer be considered to be effectively connected income. Furthermore, capital gains and most interest income are not taxed, and this rounds out the loop.

Yet the offshore fund is not the perfect solution to avoid U.S. taxation. The foreign corporation will still be subject to a withholding tax of 30 percent on dividends and certain interest. Interest on deposits with banks, savings and loan institutions, and insurance companies is exempted from withholding. As statutorily defined, portfolio interest is also exempted from withholding. Separately, offshore funds should avoid the use of money market accounts that yield dividends for the investment of cash balances. This is because the reduced 15 percent tax rate on qualified dividends is not available to foreign corporations or foreign persons subject to foreign income tax withholdings who choose not to file U.S. income tax returns.[4]

The offshore fund does provide an opportunity for U.S. tax exempts to avoid unrelated business income taxes, as it permits the use of leverage without triggering unrelated-debt financial income. Unlike onshore funds, underlying items of income and deductions do not pass through from the foreign corporations to the investor.

As the manager, you and your team are able to enjoy significant benefits from the offshore fund. There is a substantial tax deferral opportunity for you.

Just as in the onshore structure, the fund manager of the offshore structure receives two streams of fee income: management and performance fees. However, because of the nature of the company, there is a different arrangement regarding how the fees are paid. The manager receives the management fee to cover expenses. Yet since the performance fee is part of the investment management arrangement, it can be deferred for tax purposes. A cash-basis taxpayer can elect to defer the performance fee *before* it is earned and defer taxation to subsequent taxable years. The manager continues to receive tax-deferred returns on the deferred performance fee. The scheme is not available to accrual-basis taxpayers.

While deferral is a reality, questions arise about the length of the deferral agreement. Based on case law, some attorneys conservatively view 10 years as the maximum deferral period, even though there is no statutory or regulatory rule defining a maximum deferral period. Yet it should be apparent that the deferral period cannot last forever. Some attorneys take an aggressive view that additional elections to defer an already deferred performance fee before it becomes due are permissible based upon case law. However, others do not. But there is no statutory or regulatory rule that precludes a second election. An additional election involves a substantial degree of risk, constructive receipt, and immediate taxation.

While there are significant benefits to running an offshore fund, there are some potential pitfalls. Domestic money managers cannot own shares of stock in offshore corporations and an offshore fund. A domestic money manager should not be a director vested with the power to control the decisions of the offshore corporation. To some, this is a substantial problem, because even though you might foot the bill for the fund's creation, operation, and maintenance, in theory you would have little or no control over the entity. Others don't have a problem with this at all, simply because they realize that there are benefits and financial rewards to managing an offshore fund. In the end, unless you are completely comfortable with your board of directors and believe that you are protected, you should not go forward with the fund. However, if you have a satisfactory level of comfort, then it would be foolish for you not to operate an offshore fund, assuming, of course, that you can actually find assets to manage!

Marketing and Capital Raising

Before you launch your fund and create your strategy, you need to have a clear and concise marketing plan in place. Read that sentence 10 times before you go any further. Once this exercise is complete, you will be set to begin talking about how you are going to raise money and develop your business from an idea to a reality.

The purpose of this chapter is to provide you with insight into how to create, develop, and implement a marketing plan for your organization. It will provide you with case studies that explore funds that are new to the marketplace, others that are experienced in the marketplace, and a fund that faced a crisis of confidence in the marketplace. It will also give you insight into how investors will view you before, during, and after the due diligence process.

The goal here is to provide you with enough information to realize that you need to be prepared to meet with and work with investors.

The key to success in raising assets is a simple, succinct, and meaningful presentation and perseverance. Ultimately, it comes down to one word—*communication*. You need to be a great communicator. It is through communication that you will find the success and perseverance necessary for the substantial growth of your assets. I believe—and by the time you finish reading this chapter, I expect you to believe—that marketing is the most important part of a successful hedge fund operation. Some of you will gasp and ask, How can that be? The reason is simple. While being able to manage your assets and execute your strategy is clearly important to your success, without assets to manage you cannot prove that the strategy works. A car is only as good as the gasoline that makes it run. Without gasoline, you have a nice hunk of metal that collects dust and takes up space in the garage. A fund is no different, except that without assets, you will have a nice ream or two of paper as kindling for a fire when you can't pay your heating bill.

MARKETING 101

The key to your fund's short-term and long-term success will be management's marketing plan and its ability to implement it successfully. If you think that just because you built it, the assets will come, think again. The key is to create and implement a plan that will allow you to attract, maintain, and grow a solid asset base.

In Chapter 1, I explained that many people look upon marketing people in the hedge fund industry—and most of Wall Street, for that matter—to be knuckle draggers. The marketers are the people who did not go to business school or get CFA credentials, and for the most part they are thought of as Wall Street's lowest common dominator. If they bring in a lot of money, it is because the performance is so good that the product sold itself. If they don't bring in any money, they are worthless. It does not matter if the fund performed poorly for the past 6, 9, or 12 months or if the sector is in the toilet; they should be able to get some money. Or so says management. If you are going to be in charge of marketing at your firm, start listening to the tapes of the late, great Rodney Dangerfield. My friend, whether you like it or not, you will get no respect no matter what you do! If you are going to hire marketers, I would suggest that you treat them with the respect they deserve, because without them you have nothing.

Most marketers I know love what they do. Hedge fund marketing can be a lot of fun and quite rewarding, from both an ego and a financial viewpoint. You get to travel to interesting places, eat at excellent restaurants, go to swanky bars, play lots of golf, and have a really good time, all in the name of finding assets. In most cases, it pays to play this part, even if you have to put up with a lot of nonsense from your partners. As long as you keep in mind that you are the gasoline that allows the engine to run, you will be all right and might even have fun in the process.

To begin, you need to have a plan. It does not have to be 100 pages long, typed out single-spaced, but rather should provide you with a road map that will allow you to operate on a path to success. This is where most people fail, because they believe in the Kevin Costner theory that if you build it, they will come. Generally, this does not happen, and you should not rely on it for your success.

I believe that there are two rules, or lessons, that you need to subscribe to when you are planning and implementing your marketing effort.

1. Those you think will give you money when you launch your fund will most likely not invest with you right out of the gate.

2. Those you think are completely out of reach and from whom you have no chance of getting an investment may be the first people to invest in the fund.

The hedge fund business is peculiar when it comes to gathering assets. It is very hard to read investors and truly understand what they are thinking or what they are going to do until they actually tell you yes or no. Therefore, you need to truly be ready, willing, and able to market your product to everyone under the sun who is a qualified investor, because you never know where the assets are going to come from until you get the subscription documents and the wired funds.

Understanding how the process works is going to help you be more successful. In the late 1990s and the first couple of years of the new millennium, marketing consisted of playing golf, going to dinner, and having a good night out. If you could identify the investor, build a rapport, and your product was somewhat decent, in most cases wining and dining would lead to money. A lot of due diligence was done at the bar and on the phone between friends. However, as the industry has evolved, and in light of a combination of blowups and scandals, and a search for much needed alpha, investors have become more sophisticated. Alpha is the excess return on investment over the index. Consequently, the due diligence process has become more thorough and important to the investment and marketing process.

"I could take a guy to the golf course, then go to dinner and fill him with drinks, and all the while tell him what we were doing, and I was pretty much assured that he would make an investment," said one hedge fund marketer. "Today, investors still like to be wined and dined, but they also make us fill out due diligence questionnaires and ask for a lot of information before they make an investment. Investors are more serious and don't rely on the goodwill any longer."

Just a few short years ago, the hedge fund industry operated as a sort of old boy's network that relied heavily on relationships. I told you about a fund, you told me about a fund, and each of us would invest in the funds because we knew each other and trusted each other's judgment. The problem, however, was that you thought I did due diligence and I thought you did due diligence. In the end, we both were relying on other friends' tips, no due diligence was done, and we did not really know what we were getting ourselves into. Tips may get you there in the short term, but in the long term they hurt you. Period. End of story.

There are some who believe that the marketplace has become more institutionalized as large groups of pensions, endowments, and foundations have begun to invest heavily in hedge funds to meet the needs of their boards of directors. To some extent this is true, but in reality this new crop of investors just favors checking the box. If something goes wrong, they want to be able to put the blame on someone else. The problem is, managers don't mind going through this process because they believe in what Willie Sutton, the bank robber, reportedly said when asked why he robbed banks: "Because that it is where the money is."[1]

"Investors have changed. I don't know if they have gotten smarter or just seem to want to appear smarter, but now they are asking a lot more questions, and we are giving them a lot more information about our funds, our people, and our operation," said one hedge fund marketer. "I don't know if they know what to do with all the information that we give to them, but I do know that they are asking for it and that we are trying to give them whatever they want because we want their money."

THE LAZY INVESTOR

The key to your success is to remember that for the most part investors are lazy. It does not matter whether they are so-called sophisticated investors or whether they are average Joes or Janes. Both groups are inherently lazy. It is through this laziness that, as a whole, Wall Street has made a lot of money and will continue to make a lot of money. People on the Street are able to exploit this laziness to their benefit. Peter Lynch, the money manager who earned great fame and fortune running Fidelity's Magellan Fund from 1977 to 1990, said that Americans spend more time choosing their refrigerators than they do their investment portfolios. My experience tells me that Mr. Lynch is on target with this comment. However, it does not mean that investors won't request a lot of information. It just means they might not know how to use any of it.[2]

You need to be prepared. I suggest that you go online or talk to your prime broker about procuring a due diligence questionnaire. You can find an example of one at www.hedgeanswers.com. The document is a series of questions about infrastructure, strategy, risk controls, people, and financial resources. The idea is that once investors get a completed questionnaire, they have a good understanding—on paper, at least—of the size and scope of your organization. If you have one on file, you will be able to provide it to potential investors immediately upon request. If potential investors give *you* a questionnaire to fill out, you will probably be able to cut and paste the answers you already have into theirs. Either way, it will speed the process along.

CHECKING THE BOX

Today, hedge fund investing is about data points and checking boxes. The reason for this is that managers want institutional assets. Managers read stories about the California Public Employees' Retirement System (CalPERS), Massachusetts Pension Reserves Investment Management Board (MassPRIM), and every pension and foundation in between that is allocating assets to hedge funds. They want a piece of this pie.

"Everyone is chasing the big-ticket investors, because they believe that is where the money is really coming from," said a hedge fund marketing executive. "There is a lot of money coming out of these pools of assets, but in order to get it first you need to get through the consultants. And the only way to do that is to check the box."

As a hedge fund manager, the question becomes how you deal with this issue. On one hand, you don't want to do a lot of unnecessary work. But on the other hand, you need to be able to provide data points that that will allow potential investors to make an educated and thoughtful decision about your product.

The answer is simple. Present a clear and concise message, always be truthful, and listen to what the person sitting across the table is saying to you. If you put together thought-provoking, insightful material and provide good solid answers to the questions asked of you, then consider it a job well done.

"Getting a potential investor to say yes is not easy, but as long as you feel you did everything they asked of you, then you can rest easy," said the marketing executive. "The issue is listening to their requests and providing them with the material they need. After you do that, it is out of your hands."

Listening is one of the most important skills that a marketer needs to have to be successful in the hedge fund industry. Being a good listener means that you are truly interested in what investors are asking for and that you are able to provide them with the material they need to make a decision. You need to listen closely to everything the prospects are saying so that you are completely aware of what is going on with them. Be cognizant of the fact that something that seems trivial to you may be extremely important to them. If it is important to them, then it should be important to you.

To prove my point, I want to share with you a story about listening that has forever impacted my view of its importance to the sales process.

Over the past nine years or so, I have had the distinct pleasure of speaking at hedge fund conferences and programs around the world. Over this period of time, the world of hedge fund conferences has become a circuit that moves around the globe. Generally, things kick off in Florida in January, make their way to Europe by early summer, and then move on to Asia in the fall. Attending these events is fun and something that most people enjoy. I have enjoyed participating in programs with some of the most interesting people in the hedge fund business, have learned quite a lot, and made some very good friends along the way.

When I go to these events, the key for me is to learn something. I have probably been to more than 50 or 60 conferences in the past nine years. While all have unique attributes, one in particular sticks out. It's not because the venue was great or the program was fantastic, but because of something I learned from someone I truly respect and admire.

Let me set the stage.

This particular conference was in January 2002 at one of Florida's finest golf resorts. Because of the timing, the location, and a few of the speakers, the conference experienced a high turnout of hedge fund people from around the globe. The program itself was relatively mediocre, but there were a number of highlights that received significant interest from participants. One session that was packed to standing room only was a discussion by the manager of a large endowment. His topic was the asset allocation process.

This was one of only a few sessions that every hedge fund marketer and manager at the conference really wanted to attend. The managers and marketers were salivating to meet this speaker and to talk to him about their funds. They really wanted to get to this guy and his assets.

The presentation lasted for about 45 minutes and consisted of the speaker discussing the investment process that he and his team employ when allocating to hedge fund managers. He detailed the five things he looked for in a manager and the one thing that immediately turned him off. The five things that he looked for were style, assets under management, the management team, communication skills, and infrastructure. If he liked what he saw in those areas, then he moved on to the fund's track record.

He said he was happy to meet with managers and discuss their business to learn what they do and how they do it. To him, it was important that he understood the business of how the money was managed, and he liked to discuss this with them before the performance numbers. It turned him off immediately when the only thing a manager was selling was the fund's performance. "When the first words out of their mouths after hello were their fund's performance numbers, I politely excuse myself from the discussion and simply move on," he told the audience that day.

"If I am not an investor, I don't care about how a fund has done in the past. I care about how it is going to do when I do have my assets at risk," he said. "Telling me about the past does not help me understand the future, so therefore I have no interest. I want to know about style and strategy and the management team. Not how the fund did when I was not an investor."

People in the audience were taking furious notes. They were waiting with bated breath for him to finish so that they could give him their pitch. The saliva was pouring out of their mouths. And all the while, most of them forgot the most important thing. They forgot to listen to what he was saying. They were so busy trying to jockey for position after the talk that they were not listening to what he was saying, which would have helped them when they got to meet him.

I know this because later that day, when we were by the pool sipping cocktails, the speaker told me. He told me that nearly everyone who came up to him at the end of his talk began their conversations with the phrase, "My fund was up this much last year."

"The audience for the most part completely missed what I was saying, and yes, I probably will miss out on a few good managers because I immediately discounted them based on this initial encounter, but if they don't listen to what is important to me, how can I consider them?" he asked. "Listening is fundamental. And it is something we do and something we expect our managers to do."

Listening to potential and existing investors will be the key to your success. Listening will help you to understand what they need and expect from you. Listening will allow you to learn what is important to them, and listening is what will help you make sure that you are able to hold onto the assets regardless of market conditions and how the fund performs. Listening is clearly important and something that you never want to discount.

Another important aspect of marketing is to actually have the fund up and running. One problem that many new fund managers experience is their inability to get the fund up and running before they bring it to the market and talk to potential investors. These managers operate on what I call "the hope" or "the expect to" principle: when the manager tells the potential investor that they *hope* to get started by the end of the month or *expect to* be live on the first day of the month.

GETTING TO YES

A good marketing strategy begins when the fund actually starts operating, and this is the day after you decide to get into the hedge fund business. One of the most common mistakes budding hedge fund managers make is that they go around to their friends and family and other potential investors and tell them that they are getting into the business. They tell them that they are planning on starting or are working on getting the business started, but they don't seem to have a plan to actually get the fund off the ground.

Potential investors don't buy into this premarketing effort. They want to see, feel, and touch a fund before they put their money into it. Therefore, I counsel all of my clients that they need to stop telling people that they *expect to* or *hope to* get started. They need to get started immediately.

Don't tell people you are going to launch a fund. Launch it. That is our motto. Every day you are in business is one more day of track record that you build. Every day you are not in business is one less day of track record that you have to market with. The key is to get started.

This is very hard for many people to understand. They feel that they need a certain level of assets to get the ball rolling or a specific number of investors in order to launch. This is nonsense. If you are waiting for assets or investors, then you are never going to get off the ground. If you are worried about the costs of doing business, then you should stay at your job and wait until you have more money in the bank. You need to get started. That is the only way you will ever get things going. As Nike says, "Just do it!"

The question is, how does one just do it? In the previous chapters, I discussed how to get the entities up and running. Now we need to discuss how to create and implement a marketing strategy.

One of the first things you need to do is to get your story down. This should be an outline of sorts, something akin to what you did in the fifth grade. You know, no A without a B, and no 1 without a 2. Once completed, the outline will be the framework for your pitch book. It will have a beginning, a middle, and an end and will provide the potential investor with enough information about what you do and how you do it to make an educated decision about you and your product. The pitch book is not to be a selling tool that procures assets for you. That is your job. It is simply a tool that is used in the marketing process. Anyone who says a pitch book sells has sold nothing and will sell nothing. What a pitch book does is tell the story of your fund and act as a placeholder during the sales process. It allows you to stay on track and focused during your presentation, and it allows you to leave something behind at the end of the meeting. When developing your outline and the rest of your marketing material, remember the two golden rules: Keep it simple (i.e., the KISS principle), and less is more.

What you are doing is clearly high finance. At the end of the day, your version of rocket science will be that you are trying to buy something cheap and sell something expensive. Of course, the method by which you reached the decision about what to buy and sell consisted of all sorts of research and math. But when it comes right down to it, all you are doing is presuming that something will go up in value and other things will go down in value, and you position the portfolio accordingly.

The simpler the strategy, the easier it will be for investors to understand. This is the key to successful marketing. You need to be able to explain your story to them and feel confident that they understand what you are telling them. Remember to use the KISS principle in all of your communications to investors. If you don't, you will have real problems. Investors will want to understand what you are doing, and if they do not, they will not want to invest. Gone are the days when an investor took a manager's word for it. Today, investors want to know how the money is being managed. They want to know what becomes of their capital. If they can't understand it from the pitch and the pitch book, then they are going to move on. You need to keep things on a level that is easy for everyone to understand. Trust me. This will help you be more successful and raise more assets.

THE KISS PRINCIPLE

One of the best clients my firm has ever had was a start-up fund run by two guys out of UBS. The pair spent several years at Paine Webber running money and building a very lucrative business. When the firm was taken over by UBS, they decided to finish out their clients at the Swiss giant and then go out on their own. Their plan for their newfound freedom—not unlike most unemployed money managers and business development people—was to start a hedge fund. Over the years prior to the merger, the two had worked well together and had developed a successful strategy and business. They both felt it was time to go out on their own.

The pair began to meet regularly, develop a business plan, and work with service providers to get things going. During one of these sessions, they realized that they were going to need a partner with money—someone who could not only put up some working capital to cover the initial day-to-day expenses, but would also provide seed money for the fund. They determined that this person would really allow them to get off the ground faster than doing it on their own. One of the partners believed that he knew the right person, someone who would not only be willing to put up the working capital to get the business going, but who would be willing to seed the fund with a few million dollars to get things moving. An added bonus was that this individual had recently retired from another wire house after nearly 40 years, and the partners believed he would be willing to use his contacts to help them raise additional assets once things were up and running.

"It made sense for us to find a partner who had the financial wherewithal to see us through the launching and running of the fund through at least one year of operation," said one of the founding partners of the new firm. "Our job was to get the fund up and running and his was to provide financial support for our day-to-day operation and help us raise assets from his list of contacts."

One of the problems with the business plan was the marketing strategy. Without revealing names or hurting anyone's feelings, it can be said that all of the partners were extremely weak in this area. They did not understand the hedge fund business and did not understand how to go about putting together a presentation that made sense to the types of investors they needed to target. The partners came from the institutional marketplace, where more is better. They did not understand the hedge fund marketplace, where less is more. It was a hurdle that they had to overcome.

BEING AN ENTREPRENEUR

It is very difficult to be an entrepreneur. Most people who have spent a significant part, if not all, of their professional careers working at large, well-established organizations don't realize the blood, sweat, and tears that go into building a business from the ground up. And this, my dear reader, is what separates those who succeed from those who fail. The people who fail are those who refuse to adapt to the entrepreneurial way of life. Those who succeed are the ones who realize that they need to adapt and don't fight change. Thankfully, the guys in our example realized that they needed to adapt and were willing to change.

"Being an entrepreneur is hard to do, no matter what industry you are getting started in," said this hedge fund manager. "It is really hard and a lot of work to make sure all of the bases are covered. You really have to be the chief cook and bottle washer, and for a lot of people that is very hard to do."

This particular fund launch was stressful to the three partners because they did not realize how much time and effort would go into building the firm's infrastructure. They worked for quite a long time to get the documents right and to select the prime broker and accounting firm. It was a long and tedious process.

"We knew it would be hard, but we did not know how hard it was going to be," one of the partners said. "It was a lot more than simply getting a brokerage account open, depositing money and putting on a trade, and working with lawyers to get the fund documents completed."

The partners realized that they needed to raise capital. While they all had some names on a short list, it was difficult for them to get things going. One of the reasons for this was their inability to really communicate what they were doing in both print and oral presentations.

When my partner and I met with them for the first time, we spent nearly three hours listening to the strategy, learning about the infrastructure, and trying to understand what they were talking about. We found that they had a real inability to communicate what they were doing. We listened intently, took notes, and were utterly confused. Finally, I asked a question and found out that what they were doing was simply forecasting interest rates. "Simply" is not the best way to describe the strategy, because it is really not simple at all. However, when it was broken down to its barest components, it was really easy to understand.

The fund uses a proprietary method of analyzing a number of economic indicators to determine which way interest rates will head over specific time periods. It is very simple to understand once you cut through all of the nonsense. However, very sophisticated mathematical analysis and research go into the manager's investment decisions. The issue here was not whether the strategy would work, because it did. We knew this, because the partners had been using it for years at other firms. The problem was communicating the strategy to potential investors. Our job was to help them fix this. Regardless of their prior experience, we had to teach them that less is more and that keeping it simple are the keys to marketing success. It took us about six months, but in the end they got it. The fund is now doing quite well, has established a good track record, and is on course to hit $500 million in assets under management by the end of 2006. This is up from nothing just three years ago.

"We needed to refine our pitch," the manager said. "Once we understood that, we were able to communicate more effectively with potential investors and started having more success."

In marketing, success comes down to one word: *communication*. It sounds silly to some. It sounds simple to others. But it is something that most people who have done marketing believe is an absolute. Yet it is also something people lose sight of when they are launching and running a successful business. They believe that because they get it, everyone else does, too.

Communication comes down to putting together a pitch that makes sense, is easy to understand, and leaves the prospect who is getting pitched with a good understanding of what is being done and how he can profit from it.

Again, the idea is to keep it simple. You need to let people understand what you are doing, they need to believe that they are operating on your level, and they need to believe that you are worthy of their assets. You need to make sure that they understand what is happening in the fund and, most important, that they can talk to you about your fund, its strategy, and their investment without running the risk of being thought of as stupid or annoying.

"Investors like to be listened to," said one hedge fund marketing executive. "It is our job to listen to what they have to say and provide them with a platform to be heard. After all, they are our customers, and you know what they say about customers."

This may come as a shock to you, but many investors feel stupid because managers try to blind them with their investment philosophy. The idea that an investor is not smart enough to understand what is going inside an investment portfolio is ridiculous. Whenever people try to tell me how smart they are, I simply cut them off and cross them off my list. This is what other investors will do as well. Keep things simple, and you will get better results than if you try make yourself out as the smartest guy to trade the markets.

It took a lot of work, some of which is not yet complete, but the aforementioned manager has made great strides in keeping the presentation and fund materials simple and to the point. One of the partners was not used to this idea, so he has had to overcome a significant number of internal hurdles. It is difficult for him to realize that less is more. But as the fund's assets have grown, he sees the value in communicating clearly and concisely, and he is making the switch from delivering too much information to delivering just the right amount.

"It is a rude awakening for some people," said an institutional investor. "A lot of guys come out of a shop with a specific way of doing something, and they think that it is the way it is going to be in their new venture. That dog just won't hunt. You need to make sure potential investors feel like they are on your level, and the only way to do this is to adapt to your new environment."

THE OLD DAYS

A few years ago, before the scandals and blowups of 2005 and 2006, marketing was more footloose and fancy-free. The due diligence process was not as thorough, and money flowed into funds like wine. Investors relied on the word of friends or fellow investors to tell them about funds. It was like a big game of Telephone. The only difference between this game and the one we all played as kids was that at the end of the line, some investors lost a lot of money instead of just getting the message wrong.

"A lot of investors have lost faith in the industry in the last few years, as the blowups and scandals have gone from strategies that failed to out-and-out frauds," a hedge fund marketer said. "Prior to 2004 many people said that they did sophisticated due diligence but really did tertiary overviews. Now, however, because it seems that stakes are a bit higher, investors are looking for more and more information. What they are doing with it, I don't know, but I know that they are asking for it."

Collecting data and using it are two very different things. Today, it seems that no matter whom you talk to, everyone wants all sorts of information on a fund, its managers, its trading partners, and even its milk-and-coffee providers. The call for business and position transparency remains as loud as ever. Everyone wants to know everything about what is going on with a fund's people and its positions. The question I always ask is, What do they do with all this data? And while that is not necessarily your problem, you need to be able to provide them with anything and everything that they want if you really want them as investors in your fund.

It is my belief that even the most sophisticated investors are unable to process and understand position-level transparency. Yet even the most unsophisticated investors are looking for this data before they make their investment decision. Unfortunately, providing position-level data is something that you will have to deal with. It is really a shame that this is what the industry has become, because in some cases a fund is now judged by how much information it provides investors instead of the merits of its operation. While I have never been able to prove it, my belief is that the information provided to potential investors about positions and risk levels is put into a folder and becomes simply another box that is checked during the investor's due diligence process. Gathering the data allows these investors to feel good about their research efforts, and their potential investments, and, more important, it lets them feel like they have accomplished something.

"Look, when we investigate a manager, we look at three things right out of the box: who is their lawyer, who is their accountant, and who is the prime broker. If they are names that we know and names that are respected in the industry, then we move forward and go further down the due diligence process," said Richard Bookbinder, manager the Roebling fund, a New York–based fund of funds. "If we don't recognize the names or don't have any respect for the organizations that they are working with, we just kick them out of the pile and move on. It may not be the most scientific way to do it, but it is a good place to start."

It is easy to understand the value of having good service providers in your documents, not only for a fund of funds like Bookbinder's, but also for other high-net-worth and institutional investors. Regardless of size, many investors simply go through a check-the-box exercise when doing due diligence. This means that potential investors look for a few basic characteristics that they find in all funds. They continue with the due diligence process after verifying that the fund is operating and functioning with similar organizations as other funds in which they invest, meaning that the fund uses a recognizable prime broker, has a well known auditor and a law firm that has a respected hedge fund practice. As the manager being analyzed, you want to ensure that investors can check off all of their boxes, because it is silly to get hung up on items like your prime broker, lawyer, or accountant, when there are so many reputable organizations offering services to the industry.

As discussed in Chapter 1, you need to work with service providers who are experienced and well regarded in the hedge fund industry. Many people know lawyers who can probably write the documents for you. Let's face it, writing hedge fund documents is not rocket science, and all of us know a local CPA. However, when you are meeting with potential investors, they are going to look for names they recognize—the same names they have seen in other funds they have invested in or are performing due diligence on. If they don't see names they recognize, you are potentially going to lose out on their assets.

This is probably the easiest hurdle you will face during the due diligence process. You definitely do not want to be spending time with potential investors explaining why you chose one lawyer or one accountant over another. You just want to show them who you are working with and move on.

THE VALUE OF SERVICE PROVIDERS

One reason many investors put a lot of weight in the service providers is because they believe that if a respected law firm, accountant, or prime broker is willing do to business with the fund, then the fund must have passed some level of due diligence. To these investors, this is an important first step in their investment process. While having service providers who are recognizable is important, it is also important to have a clear and concise explanation of your style, strategy, and how you got to where you are today.

A number of years ago, my partner and I were at a due diligence meeting with a manager based in Westchester, New York. We went to the manager's office and spent the afternoon learning about his fund, his organization, and his background in the securities and money management business.

One of the things I like to do when talking to new managers is to get a feel for where they came from. I don't mean prior jobs. I mean their childhood and their upbringing. I ask them questions about high school, the sports they played, and the activities they participated in, and then I move on to college, and so forth.

This specific manager told us quite a bit about his family and his experience at a local high school and his effort to get into a good college. He told us that he went to an Ivy League college on a need-based scholarship. To me this meant that he had the academics to get into the school but did not have the financial resources to pay for the education. I thought this was great. In my book, it meant a lot and told me that he was probably very smart and very hungry. Two characteristics I like in a potential manager! Check that box!

About a half hour later, after discussing his college days and the early part of his career on the Street, we started talking about the fund and how it got started. He told us that the fund was seeded by his family, approximately $10 million right out of the gate.

Something did not smell quite right. I asked him how this was possible. If the family had $10 million to invest in his fund, why and how did he qualify for a need-based scholarship? To this question, he had no answer. He told us that he preferred not to discuss it and that he wanted to move on. I agreed and thanked him for his time. Needless to say, we did not invest with this manager.

To our chagrin, the manager has done extremely well. He has more than $300 million in assets under management and has built a successful business. Maybe we made a mistake by not investing with him, but I don't think so. Something did not and does not smell right with this guy. There are plenty of good managers out there, and the key is to find ones that you can be completely comfortable with. We were not comfortable with him or his story, so we took a pass.

As a new manager or as an existing manager looking for more assets, you need to avoid situations such as the preceding one. You need to be able to say, "This is my story, and I am sticking to it." It sounds funny, but as I wrote this, I kept thinking that the key is to be able to communicate in a clear, concise, and truthful manner. You need to be able to tell people who you are and what you do in a simple form. They need to believe they can get their arms around what you are doing and can have faith in you and your team's ability to manage money. If you have skeletons in your closet, you don't need to wear them on your sleeve. But if you are asked about them, tell the truth. Everybody makes mistakes, and everybody has issues. Those who know how to admit their mistakes and deal with their issues are the ones I want to do business with. Investors realize that you are human. They are willing to work with you to help you be successful. Your job is to search them out.

The search for investors is a difficult one. It is something that many believe is easy. But I am here to tell you, it is quite difficult. You need to be focused. As a single-manager fund, you need to do the following exercise to ensure success.

First, you need to put together a list of everyone you know who you believe has the ability to invest in your fund. Second, you need to put together a list of all the potential outlets for your fund, such as institutions, endowments, and funds of funds that may have some interest. Third, you need to cast the widest net possible to reach people in all corners of the world. The idea is to get in front of as many people as possible to see whether they have an interest in what you are doing. The key to this exercise is numbers. The more people you hit, the greater the success you will have in finding assets. This is why marketers are the knuckle draggers. Because in its most basic form, there is literally no difference between trying to raise money for a hedge fund and selling magazine subscriptions door-to-door. The key is numbers. Get in front of enough people and you are bound to find someone who will have an interest in what you are doing. Once you find money, you will find it a lot easier to find more money. The hurdles are easier to get over as your assets grow.

The issue comes down to what you are willing to do to be successful. Most people believe that they are above aggressively marketing their products. Most people believe that the money will come into their fund simply because they built it. Here is a harsh reality: Investors don't need you; you need them.

HUNGER IS KEY

You need to be focused. You need to be hungry. And you need to be aggressive. You also need to stick to the rules, which means no outward advertising and no soliciting anyone you don't know or who does not come to you first. Therefore you need to be creative. You need to look for ways to meet and get exposed to as many potential investors as possible. It is important to try to exploit connections you have with friends, former colleagues, and acquaintances in order to gain access to potential investors. There is nothing wrong with asking people you know for introductions; it is expected and acceptable. It is trench warfare. Man, does this sound hard. Well, guess what. It is! My only advice is be prepared for failure, because that is what will lead you to success. There is an old saying that things are at their darkest just before the dawn. In my experience of working with new and existing hedge funds, this has been proven true time and time again.

Over the past few years, my partner and I have worked hard to help a number of managers get over certain problems they were experiencing with their marketing efforts. During this time, we have tried to come up with strategies and ideas that will help them better understand what they are doing wrong and provide them with a knowledge base to be more successful in the marketplace. One of the first things we have told people is not to be too proud.

As the industry has grown significantly during these past few years, it has faced a number of obstacles. We have found that many managers have been unwilling to adapt or change according to investor demands. As I wrote earlier in this chapter, most investors are looking for, and sometimes requiring, position-level transparency, reduced fees, and specific liquidity provisions. Most existing fund managers are not willing to give an inch, while many new managers are willing to give it all.

We have seen significant resistance by some managers who question the need to provide special treatment to investors. I have been on the receiving end of e-mails that question why investors want this sort of treatment and whether they are worth it. My response is always the same: If it is not too much trouble, give in to their requests. If it is too much trouble, then find a way to make it *not* too much trouble and give it to them. In the end, my friend, the customer is always right! Special treatment seems to be the request du jour of investors who want to enter funds that have had a problem or have experienced difficulty and are on their way back up the ladder.

We happen to be very close to a fund that experienced some rough times over the past few years. It posted poor performance and significant turnover. The owner of the company, who has done fabulously well by anyone's standards, decided that he was not finished and that he wanted to bring the firm back to its glory days. He was willing to put the effort and finances into the firm to make this a reality, regardless of cost or effort.

Over the years, the firm had gotten slightly lazy in its marketing efforts. It had also taken a snobbish attitude toward raising capital. During its heyday, the fund's manager really let things go. Part of the problem was the size of the organization, part of it was leadership, and part of it was the inability of its marketing people to deal with real marketing issues. The firm had adopted the attitude that it didn't care whether certain people invested money in it, because if they didn't, someone else would.

"We were bogged down in an environment that allowed us to take a guy out to dinner, play some golf with him, and buy him some drinks, and we were assured a nice investment because the guy did not want to get caught without us in his portfolio," said the firm's managing partner. "We literally were selling water in the desert, everybody wanted in, and we were willing to take them as long as we liked the size of the investment. We had a fund that everybody wanted."

However, as performance started to go south and people started to leave, the marketplace developed jitters about the firm and management realized that the investors that they thought needed them were now needed by the fund.

"We did not cultivate or manage our relationships properly," the manager said. "Instead of selling water in the desert, we were trying to sell ice to Eskimos, and that was something that we were not prepared or quite qualified to do. It was something we did not have experience in."

This inability to manage the customer/investor relationship was the partial cause for massive withdrawals from the firm. Quite literally, redemptions by a few caused a run on the bank. And the withdrawals had a deep effect on the funds, its managers, and its infrastructure.

"We were dumbfounded by what we saw happening," said one member of the firm's marketing team. "We could not believe how much money was being moved out of the funds and how fast the redemption notices were coming in."

To weather this storm, the firm began to operate with a bunker mentality. The managers began to meet with investors to preempt their withdrawal notices. They were trying to prove that they were worthy of the client money that they still had in their coffers.

"The idea was to get a story to them about what we were doing and how we were going to survive in order to ensure that the money would stay with the firm and not go out the door," the manager said. "In some cases it worked, in other cases, we failed miserably."

In the end, the firm saw its assets drop by nearly 50 percent over a one-year period. Yet during this time, the fund was up nearly 11 percent. The one thing that it proved to its investors and the world was that its money management team was strong enough to make money regardless of the outflows and market conditions. This is something that the firm has since used in their efforts to rebuild its asset base.

"We were involved in the perfect storm," said the manager. "We were hit on all sides, but I think what hurt us the most was when people on the inside turned against us and people on the outside started listening to what they were saying."

The firm has survived. One of the first things the manager did was to let go of a significant amount of deadweight in the marketing department. He cut off the arm to save the body. This caused some initial problems in the marketplace. In the long run, the marketplace seemed to understand that it was necessary for the firm's survival.

"When your own marketing people refuse to talk to investors or prospect, it is a problem," said the manager. "It is even more of a problem when the Street finds out about it. The hedge fund industry is a very small place, and the word gets out quickly. How can you expect outsiders to have confidence in you when insiders don't?

"These are the things we had to deal with and it was hard," he continued. "We had to make tough choices, but we are better for it. We are stronger now than before, and we will survive."

The firm made a number of adjustments to staff and overhead and worked hard to get the message out that not only was it here to stay, but that it was very committed to the business. It took the fund company about a year to turn things around. Now the tide has turned, and the business seems to be back on track.

The reality is it that it comes down to self-confidence. If you have the financial wherewithal and the belief in your product and its sustainability, then you have a chance. If you don't believe in it, then it does not matter how much money you have. You should fold the tent and go home.

As a new fund starting out, it is critical that you have the financial wherewithal to get through the lean times. I suggest that if you do not have in the bank at least three times the amount you earned in your best year working for someone else, then you are probably going to have a tough time making it through the first few years of being out on your own.

Remember that very few funds start up and launch with hundreds of millions or billions of dollars. You may read in the popular press about those who do launch with hundreds of millions or more in assets. But in reality, these examples are few and far between. For the most part, new funds start with assets under $100 million. This means that not only do you, as the manager, need to cover the operating expenses of both the fund and the organization out of your own pocket, but you will not be drawing a salary. Therefore, you need to be able to cover your living expenses. You will need to have significant amounts of cash in the bank. Questions about your rainy-day fund are going to come up during the due diligence process. Most seasoned, institutional, high-net-worth investors are cognizant of this issue and will ask you about it. If you are prepared, then they will know you are serious about your endeavor. If you appear not to have thought of or prepared for any eventuality, they will question your sustainability.

"I expect a manager to tell me that they are prepared to not take any salary or money out of the business for the first couple years," said one doctor who invests in hedge funds for his family office. "My experience is that for the most part, funds that succeed are those in which the manager and his team are prepared for the worst. If a manager gives a blank stare when I ask this question, it tells me that they are not prepared for the worst and it is probably a fund that I am not going to go with. I like managers who think of everything or at least try to cover all of their bases."

As I said at the beginning of this chapter, the goal of these 9,300-odd words is to provide you with enough information to attack your marketing effort with gusto. It is to make you understand that just because you have a bunch of rich friends, you may not succeed in getting them to invest in your fund. And that no matter how big you become, without investors you are nothing. I hope that has come across in these pages. To see examples of marketing presentations that I believe work well, go to www .hedgeanswers.com.

CHAPTER 7

Why the Back Office Matters

As you continue to build your business, one of the first things you will realize is that you need to make sure your infrastructure is good and solid. Your operation's infrastructure and how it appears will become a major part of the success of your business. Investors truly like to kick the tires. They do so not only by looking at your marketing and performance material, but also by viewing your office space, computers, and human resources. While it is important to put on a good show, you must also ensure that you have all the tools you need to be successful.

USING THE RIGHT TOOLS

Having the right tools at your disposal is important. Doing so will allow you not only to build your business, but also to maintain an edge in the markets. With today's advances in technology, all of the information you need to make a decision about a potential investment is probably just a mouse click away. While this is viewed as good by some, I believe it is actually bad and makes a manager's job harder. The Internet and its resources, combined with the development of Bloomberg and Reuters machines, have truly leveled the playing field. The technological advances of just a few short years have provided us with the ability to trade from anywhere we have access to the Internet. However, your competitors have access to everything that you do. All of the same information, all at the same time, is available to everyone who wants it and is willing to pay for it. Remember that while you are using technology to make better, more efficient investment decisions, so are the funds you are competing against.

Therefore, your job as a manager has and will become more difficult—sometimes before you have even launched your fund. The days of picking off the low-hanging fruit are over. You can thank the Internet and the mayor of New York for that. The question is, how are you going to get and maintain your edge?

Right out of the gate—even before you make it to the gate—you need to think about developing and maintaining an edge. Let's face it, you would not be willing to put up the money and go through the motions of putting the business together if you did not think you had an edge. What you need to do is to define, massage, and master it. (By the way, your edge is how you are going to make money.)

Once it is defined and in place, you need to determine how to maintain it. Undoubtedly, your strategy will rely on your ability to retrieve and process information. Some people need to do it with great speed; others do it with great volumes of material; and a third group just needs to do it. You will figure out what works best for you and then you need to figure out how to implement infrastructure that will allow you to do it. When it comes to using technology for gathering and processing data, most people think of using sophisticated number-crunching algorithms. My belief is that this is generally not necessary. I believe in making things simple. This means using commonly found tools to do uncommon things. News trackers that are free on Yahoo! and Google are often a great first line of defense. You allow them to do all the heavy lifting and then wait for the material to arrive. A number of times something will pop up on my screen from one of the trackers that is so obscure that I would never have found it through my conventional methods. Yet by doing nothing, I receive it almost as fast as it happens. The key is setting up the parameters on your filters to make sure the trackers find what you need. This is important for two reasons: (1) It is free, and (2) it takes little or no effort to retrieve this information that otherwise may have required you to review hundreds or thousands of articles to find.

As a start-up manager, you need to keep your costs in line with your business plan, and you need to maximize your ability to gather information efficiently. Many start-up firms I have talked to report that they are big proponents of the free sites offered through Yahoo! Finance and Bloomberg. These sites allow their people to gather data and do research without any cost. You do not need to reinvent the wheel, but you do need to figure out how to make that wheel most efficient for you.

Just as the hedge fund industry has grown over the past few years, so has the cost of technology for a start-up hedge fund. It is sometimes difficult to justify buying services from multiple data providers. The cost of a Bloomberg, a Pertrac license, and access to a Reuters machine often is more expensive than renting an office! As the manager, you need to determine what your needs really are and then build your infrastructure around them. Remember that *wants* are important, but *needs* are usually critical to the success of the business.

When it comes to developing your infrastructure, your prime broker will tell you that it is going to help you. In reality, the firm will not be able to do too much in the way of infrastructure advancement. Prime brokers are about making money, and while they have all of the tools and services you need, these things come at a price. Therefore, you must shop around to ensure that your prime broker is giving you the best price on executions and on the technology offered as part of its service to your fund. It is not to your benefit to become accustomed to taking whatever the prime broker is giving. It will end up costing you more than necessary in additional fees and commissions.

THE BEGINNING

In the beginning, you need to sit down with your partners and look at how you trade, look at what markets you trade, and decide what tools you need to be successful. You need to look at where the information flow comes from and how that information is processed. The way to do that is to determine which tools you are using at your current place of employment or even at your house and then figure out what you plan to use when you are on your own. Most likely, the bulk of the work you are doing is being done through software found on standard issues of Microsoft Office. You may be gathering the data from a Bloomberg terminal. But probably you are crunching it through Excel and other tools in that suite of Microsoft products.

When it comes to Bloomberg, keep in mind that Bloomberg is not about doing any one thing really well. It is about doing many things at an acceptable level. The beauty of the Bloomberg machine is that it can tell you the price of a vintage bottle of Château Mouton Rothschild or offer up the entire history of the 30-year Treasury bond. You may need both or you may need neither. Nonetheless, the question is, Do you need a Bloomberg? Only you and your partners can answer that question. Get what you need, not what you think you need. Technology is good, but good research is better. And the best research for hedge fund managers comes from the computer between their ears.

Your infrastructure should be built around making you the most efficient money manager possible. Obviously, you are going to need a couple of personal computers loaded with the basics, and probably Microsoft Office or a similar suite of programs, because you will need to be able to pump out documents and crunch numbers. You are also going to need a data feed, which generally will be provided by your prime broker. This will be a desktop icon that gives you real-time access to the markets. You can get this from other brokers you trade with as well. These services and systems will give you access to pretty much all of the analytics you need to do basic quantitative analysis.

After the trade is made, you will need to rely on your prime broker, who will provide you with trade blotters and portfolio management software that will allow you to see the full picture of your portfolio at all times. All of this information should be available in a real-time, online environment. The prime broker's platform is something that you will become very accustomed to using and something that will allow you to truly keep score and stay abreast of what is going on with every position in your portfolio. One piece of software that has been of great use to me and my organization is Advent Geneva, which is a global portfolio accounting system that gives us the real-time information we need to determine exactly where we stand with our investments. The software is used by our prime broker and integrates all of our orders and our money flows. It provides performance data with a few clicks of the mouse. With this software, we can see all of our positions at all times and understand the profits and losses from those transactions, as well as margin balances.

As the use of technology has evolved on Wall Street, most prime brokers have developed very sophisticated Web-based reporting functions and real-time execution systems. You need to first determine the best way for you to execute your orders. Most likely, it is going to be through a screen from your prime broker. Then you should find other ways to execute your orders, in the event that you do not like the prices you are seeing on the screen or there is a difficult order to get done.

Today, as prices come down and the industry moves away from soft dollars, there is an abundance of people offering execution services to hedge fund managers. It pays to shop around for the best price and the best service. It is also important to make sure that you have multiple outlets to execute your orders, because at the end of the day you want to make sure that you can get the orders done the way you want them. I always suggest that a new fund, regardless of size, open multiple accounts with prime brokers to ensure that you are getting the best execution and the products and services you need to be successful.

THE OFFICE

When it comes to setting up the office, you are going to need to buy computers, a fax machine, a copy machine, and other office equipment to make the office run smoothly. However, if you are using an office within a hedge fund hotel, most of the equipment you need will be provided by the prime broker. For a fee tacked onto your rent, you will be up and running. My experience in setting up an office is that less is more when it comes to technology, furniture, and other office accoutrements. One of the problems our society has today is that we always want the latest and greatest technology. We believe that if we are not on the cutting edge, we will find ourselves on the bleeding edge.

A brief story will prove my point. In 1991, I had the pleasure of working for IBM as the on-campus representative at Clark University. My job was to educate staff and students about IBM personal computers and sell them to the community. It was difficult. IBM was selling the PS2, and its top competitor was Apple. For every IBM that I sold, there were probably 10 Apples being sold on campus. It was an incredibly uphill battle. Although it was something I thoroughly enjoyed, it also proved to be very frustrating. No one saw the value of the PS2 or the IBM Microsoft operating system. On the contrary, it seemed that everyone saw the beauty and ease of the Mac. During this process, however, I learned something very interesting about technology and the way the market bought it. I learned that 90 percent of the time, people bought technology well above their real needs, simply because they wanted the latest and greatest machine. They did not care that they were going to use it for simply outputting papers and going online. They wanted the power! Consequently, these people were willing to spend $3,000 to $4,000 for a machine that could process and deliver significantly more data and run more programs than they needed. Unfortunately for me, I was on a fixed commission. So it did not matter whether they bought the expensive one or the cheap one. I got the same $40 commission, regardless of the size of the sale and the price of the computer. However, it did teach me a good lesson: When you are buying technology, write down everything you are planning to do with it and figure out exactly what you need before making the purchase. Less is more.

While purchasing technology is important, it is more important to have someone who is able to service it. When the machine fails, the last thing you want to do is dial a toll-free tech-support line and hope to get through to someone who can help you. You need to stay focused on your business and let someone else focus on the technology and its problems. It is very, very important that you have a reliable organization that can provide you with good services and support to make sure your needs are met before, during, and after problems occur.

As I wrote in Chapter 1 of this book, one of my favorite stories of the entrepreneurial side of being a hedge fund manager is Nancy Havens's comparison of her interaction with tech support at Bear Stearns and her experience after opening her own firm and realizing there was really no one to call. She then became the head of tech support.

Today, we are so technology-dependent that you must commit resources, time, and energy to having good, solid technology resources at your disposal. This does not mean you need to hire your own on-site tech person, but it does mean you need to contract with a company that can provide you with the services you need in an efficient and timely manner.

Going through the process of setting up your fund and your firm can be a lot of fun . . . as well as extremely stressful and painful. One of the best parts of the exercise is coming up with a name for your company and its funds. There are great stories on Wall Street about how names of funds came about and where they were chosen. Many are simple. For example, SAC Capital Partners comes from Steven A. Cohen, the company's founder and principal. Soros Management comes from its founder, George Soros. Tiger Management came from Julian Robertson's son, who told his father that he thought the name was easy to remember, since Julian called people Tiger. Names come from all sources: trees, streets, squares, and even folk heros. A friend of mine named his fund of funds the Roebling Fund, after the engineer, designer, and builder of the Brooklyn Bridge, John A. Roebling. The key is finding a name that is not taken, that makes sense, and that is easy to use in marketing material, e-mail, and on the Web.[1]

When it comes to building your Web presence, you are really on your own. I am not a firm believer in the Web. I view it as little more than inter-active television that shuts your mind off. However, my firm has a Web site, and I suggest that yours should as well. Today, one of the first things sophisticated and institutional investors are going to do is to Google you. They will search for your name, your partners' names, and the name of your company to see what information comes up. You, too, should run this search from time to time to ensure that you know what is being said about you on the Web. Again, I believe that less is more, and this axiom will serve you well in the long run, too. Investors are not looking for sites with bells and whistles or the most up-to-date Web design. They are looking for simple, concise sites that are easy to navigate. You should provide enough information to get them interested in learning more about you and your fund.

It is extremely important that you operate your own e-mail servers. Initially, you will think that this is a hassle and not worth it, especially if there are just two of you. However, e-mail is a mission-critical function that cannot be left to someone else. You should also run your own phones. However, this is a little more difficult if you are working in someone else's office or in a hedge fund hotel.

If something goes wrong, you know who to blame and you can begin to fix it immediately. It is much easier for you to work with your own people to solve problems quickly than to wait in line for someone else's help. If you are using someone else's network or server, at the end of the day you are going to be at their whim. When something goes wrong, you will have to wait until they want to work with you to get things fixed. Remember, what is important to you is not necessarily important to someone else, but if they are on your payroll, it will be very important to them. The key to success is communication, and you need to make sure that your tools are always working.

INSURANCE

Another thing you need to think about is insurance. Insurance is a pain in the neck, but it is a necessary evil. You will need to get a health insurance plan, a property and casualty plan, a workers' compensation plan, and perhaps directors' and officers' insurance. It is a nightmare, a bloody nightmare. There is no other way to describe it. Why? First, insurance is a sunk cost with no potential revenue. Second, the application process is a hassle, and you and your colleagues probably know little about buying insurance, so it will be like flying blind in a snowstorm. Tread very carefully when it comes to insurance. You need to make sure you are working with people you can trust, people who will give you good advice and offer the best solutions, in both products and costs, for your needs.

Insurance is generally not something most start-up managers think about when they are discussing launching a business or working on the documents. Most people just assume that it will be there. Unfortunately, that is not the case. In fact, it is very difficult to deal with, especially if you have a family. Health insurance can be an enormous expense for a start-up company, but it is one of those things that you cannot be without. If you can, a good option is to use COBRA, because that program will last 18 months and can provide a good stopgap solution to going out and getting your own plan. The problem comes when you hire people for your firm. They are going to need some coverage and will expect you to pay for at least a portion of it. It is very important to get multiple bids when you are seeking a health insurance provider. You may find that you can get similar coverage for substantially lower prices, depending on the carrier and whether the broker can tweak a plan. This is very important, especially if you have multiple employees. I know from our own experience. Some employees have families, some do not. As a result, our insurance bill is a significant portion of our monthly infrastructure expense and something we pay very close attention to when it comes time for renewal.

Along with health insurance, something that you will definitely need and *cannot* overlook is your workers' compensation policy. Most states make it very easy for you to get this coverage, and it becomes something you do not think about. However, if you do not get the coverage, be prepared to pay significant fines. A number of states, including New York, Connecticut, and New Jersey, do not look favorably upon companies that do not have plans in place. However, if it is just you and your partner, you will not need a policy. As soon as you hire an employee, you will need to have the coverage.

Payroll is something else that you will need figure out. Initially, if it is just you and your partner, as members of the LLC you are not allowed to draw a salary and will be compensated through distributions. However, if you have an analyst or administrator, you will need to be able to pay them. Thankfully, payroll services are a dime a dozen. The market is extremely competitive, and, as the consumer, you can easily play two against the middle to lower the price for the services you need. You cannot and should not do payroll yourself. You need to have a payroll company. It is another one of those things that you will need to figure out as the firm begins to take shape and operate.

The best thing to do is to make a checklist. We have a checklist available online at www.hedgeanswers.com. Using a checklist will help you stay focused, and it will keep you on track and allow you to be more efficient.

Under no circumstances should you lose focus on the fact that establishing good infrastructure is the first step to running a successful business. Infrastructure includes all of the stuff that allows you to run your business. It means the telephones, computers, fax machines, Internet connections, insurance, rent, lights, gas, electric, and water for your bathrooms. It also means cable television, because you are going to want to have a TV on in your office that has CNBC, CNN, or whatever is available in your area.

You must stay focused on what is important. I know of one fund that, once it raised significant assets, bought a large flat-screen television for the conference room. Today, this is commonplace on Wall Street—and in most companies' conference rooms, for that matter. But what was unique about this particular situation was the amount of time one of the principals spent researching and testing the set. I thought it was quite a waste of time. In the end, the sets in these rooms are used infrequently and generally are tuned to one or two channels. It really doesn't matter what make or model it is, only that it works. Get it done and move on. That is what an entrepreneur does. Don't become bogged down in the minutiae.

To avoid hassles when setting up infrastructure, establish a budget for office expenses and stick to that budget. Sit down and say, "Okay, we are going to spend X dollars on furniture, X dollars on technology, X dollars on televisions, X dollars on this, and X dollars on that." Then you need to commit to the budget and stick with it, no matter what!

HIRING PEOPLE

Currently, a glut of jobs is available in the hedge fund market for those who have accounting backgrounds. Administrators, accounting firms, and even some hedge funds are hiring them. If you go to village.albourne.com, Careerbuilder.com, Monster.com, or any of the other sites listing jobs in the hedge fund market, you will find hundreds of advertisements looking for finance and accounting people. Firms are looking for people who are CPAs or who have similar backgrounds, people who can process the numbers and deal with the financial side. You do not need to hire a full-time CFO or accountant right out of the gate. You can get away with using a part-time bookkeeper and taking advantage of the services your prime broker offers. Unfortunately for many applicants, this seems to be the only group of people being sought today. For the most part, that is good news for the start-up manager. You can take advantage of this because many people are looking for trading, marketing, and analyst positions, and the fruit is ripe for the picking. You should focus on hiring a good, solid office manager/administrator. This person can be someone who does not necessarily have a background in the hedge fund industry, but should be someone who has good people and organizational skills and who is thorough. You need someone who is dedicated and focused, and who really wants to work and seize the opportunity before them. You need to find competent people. In my experience, it is a mistake to hire people just because of their background. If they are coming from a big corporate environment, it will be difficult for them to adjust to a small organization. They will not like it, and they will not thrive. You need to hire competent people who have an entrepreneurial spirit. It is a difficult task. There really is no good way to hire people. Sometimes you need to go with your gut.

Currently, there is a glut of high-priced people in the hedge fund market looking for jobs. This is typically the case in the early spring and early fall. In the early spring, people know what their bonuses are, they have been paid, and they are usually unhappy. So they look for a change. They think that the grass is greener elsewhere and go out to look for a new job. In the early fall, there is a glut of people looking for work because they see that they are not going to make their numbers and won't get a good bonus. Therefore, they want to make a switch before the end of the year. The reality of the situation is that there are always people looking for jobs in the hedge fund world, and you need to find people who are competent and who believe in what you are building.

I often suggest that people hire people they know and have observed in the workplace and who can potentially lead to other good hires. For example, when we were launching our company, one of the first people we hired was someone who had been an administrator for us in a prior company. This person had a good background and was reliable and trustworthy. We knew the person's strengths and weaknesses and that her abilities matched what we needed. We knew she would be a great fit for us. Our next hire was a graduate student. This person was fantastic. She was looking for part-time work while she was working on her master's degree, and she turned out to be an asset to the organization.

Over the past few years, we have learned that two of the most important things to stay focused on during the hiring process are your resources and how that person is going to use them once on board. You need to manage your resources. You do not want to spend your time educating people. You do not want to spend a lot of your time monitoring them to see whether they are making personal calls or not handling things correctly.

When it comes to the person who is going to answer your phone, you have to remember that this will be the voice of your company. If that person is unprofessional, unpleasant, unkind, and/or a poor speaker, then you are going to look like an idiot and be deemed unprofessional by the people who call your office. You cannot afford to have this happen. Remember, you get to make a first impression only once, so it has to be right. The person who answers the phone says a lot about your company and the firm's level of and commitment to professionalism.

Your first hire will probably be your office manager/administrator. This is an important hire because the person is going to take a lot of the pressure of the day-to-day operation off of you. You need to hire someone you trust, someone who is reliable, and somebody who drinks the company's Kool-Aid. You are correct. It should remind these new employees of Jones. If you don't understand what I mean by this, e-mail me at das@hedgeanswers.com and I will explain.

In terms of headhunters, over the past few years there has been enormous growth in the number of people focused on finding jobs in the hedge fund industry for other people. As you can imagine, headhunters have realized that the hedge fund industry is exploding. And as it explodes, there are lots of people who not only are in need of work, but who want to work and therefore have built a business around people needing work. As with any industry, there are good headhunters and there are bad. Our experience with headhunters is that they generally look for the easy way out. They look for the person who seems to be the perfect candidate so they can minimize the amount of work they have to do with the client. They are not interested in stories. They want to fit a round peg into a round hole and don't care about anything else. We have had very little luck with headhunters over the years. I think that for the most part they just don't get it.

Most of our hiring success has come from using Monster.com. We have had great success with that Web site and will continue to use it. The headhunters who focus on the hedge fund industry are not able to handle entry-level positions or are not looking for people who have little or no experience. They are really trying to put in place a lot of accountants, administrators, and high-end jobs. Headhunters are perfect for a large organization looking for a head of marketing, head of product development, or head of prime broker sales. We have found that our needs are in an area of the market in which headhunters are not focused. The few hedge funds we know of that use headhunters are looking for an in-house accountant, a chief financial officer, maybe even a chief operating officer.

Most hedge funds are not looking for people through headhunters. Those that do use headhunters are generally looking for a CFO or a chief operating officer. If you are in need of someone for such a position, then I suggest that you go to Google and type in "headhunter" and "hedge fund" and see what comes up.

THE BUSINESS

When it comes to setting up the business, you need to think about what I call "the way things are done."

"The way things are done" constitutes the processes that you put in place that allow your business to function efficiently. You need to pay attention to a hundred little things when you are setting up and running a business.

Following is a list of things that you and your employees are going to need to be cognizant of. You will need to have policies and procedures in place for dealing with these as your business grows:

- Investors
- Potential investors
- Documents
- Performance results
- Brokers
- Administrators
- Banks/custodians

These items are the front line and the rear and need to be looked after. I know it sounds silly and you might think that it is not important, but trust me, by paying attention to the seven areas listed here, your firm will be stronger and more successful. You need to make sure that you are focused on these items:

- Make sure that you communicate properly to your investors.
- Make sure that you communicate properly to potential investors.
- Keep a log of all the documents that you send out.
- Keep all your data in one place for easy access, and make sure that you have a point person who will traffic all material.

The reason you need to do this is twofold. First of all, you want to make sure you are doing everything that you are required to do under current and future regulations. Second, you need to make sure that any and all documents you send out are the right ones. As I stated earlier in this chapter, you can make a first impression only once. Therefore, make sure you make the right impression the first time; to accomplish this, you need to have someone who traffics all your documents. This stuff may sound basic, right? I am here to tell you that it is not easy. It is very time-consuming. And it is frustrating. It is the reason you need to appoint someone competent and qualified to get the job done right the first time.

A friend of mine runs a small fund of funds in midtown Manhattan. He has a great person working for him. She collects data and documents, she processes documents, and she does a super job. By doing her work well, she allows him to stay focused on his priorities—making investments for his investors and talking to investors and potential investors. But the point of my story is this: You need to delegate some of your activities to make you more efficient. By being more efficient, you will be more successful.

This chapter is called "Why the Back Office Matters" because it is about the things that you need to do to build a successful business. You need to be cognizant of the fact that everything discussed in this chapter is part of the bigger picture, which is your ability to raise and manage assets. By having the right infrastructure and by focusing on the others, your life will be easier, your company will be more stable, and your organization will be stronger.

CHAPTER 8

The Launch

In life, very few decisions are more difficult than deciding to become an entrepreneur. It takes guts, a strong belief in your abilities, and money. The first two are easier to come by than the third.

Wall Street, however, makes it very easy for people to take the plunge. First, it provides you with the stories of those who did it before you and became wildly successful and extremely rich. Then it gives you all of the tools you need to build your business with the click of the mouse. In the end, what will allow you to go out on your own will be the desire and need to win. To win in the hedge fund business means that you have built a fund complex that puts up good numbers and attracts significant assets. It may sound easy, but it is extremely difficult. I am sure you can be successful. The real question is whether you believe that you will be successful.

Only you can answer that question. If you hesitate and say that you think so, then my suggestion is to stop reading this book and go back to working for someone else. If you answer yes, then you should absolutely read on. You know in your gut whether it is the right decision, and you have to be brutally honest with yourself. Remember that the gut never lies.

Taking the plunge and going for it will be simultaneously exhilarating, exciting, and extremely difficult. But in the end, it will be worth it.

Unlike opening a dry cleaner, pretzel stand, or bookstore, the hedge fund world is a complete enigma in the world of entrepreneurs. There is no other industry I know of in which two people in an apartment can be in business in a matter of weeks and be making money almost immediately. The barriers to entry are low, and that is a good thing.

The reason most people are interested in going into the hedge fund business is not the glory that comes with picking winners, but the financial rewards paid to those who pick the winners. I am a big opponent of the way the popular press writes about this industry and believe that most of the time they get it wrong. However, there is one thing that they write about correctly, and that is the amount of money that some of the best and brightest managers make on an annual basis.

This is why you bought this book and why you are immediately going to set up a meeting with a lawyer and accountant. This is why deep down you want to get into the hedge fund business. You want to make money, and lots of it.

Don't get me wrong. I am in it for the money as well. Believe me when I tell you that nearly everyone you talk to will say that deep down, in their heart of hearts, that is why they are hedge fund managers. The money and the fun that go along with a successful business make it all worthwhile.

Running a hedge fund will allow you to have a lot of fun managing your assets and your business. The best part of it all is that at the end of the day it is yours. You will reap what you sow. There is nothing wrong with thinking about the money and the rewards that come with the success of building a good business. It is the American way. It is what should motivate you, drive you to do the research on potential investments, and go out and raise capital. It is through this work that you will succeed. Being a hedge fund manager is like having a license to print money. The only issues are figuring out how to get the ink and where to get the paper. If you can get these two things down, it is yours to mess up!

THE PLAN

Once you have made the decision to go out on your own, you need to put together a road map that details your plan for building your business, raising assets, and managing your portfolio. I am not a huge believer in extensive and thorough business plans, but I also do not believe that you can just shoot from the hip and be successful.

My experience has been that the people who write thorough and thought-provoking business plans usually fail gracefully, while those who shoot from the hip crash like the *Hindenburg*. Therefore, you need to come up with what I call "the happy medium" of business plans. Your job is to put together a plan that is thorough yet flexible. It should allow you to adapt to situations that arise whenever you start a project and you don't know exactly where it is going to finish. This is my advice to anyone who is leaving a job and going out on his or her own with a relatively small amount of money: You will need a plan to be successful. Today, most fund managers launch with somewhere between zero and $25 million in assets under management. These are not the funds you read about in the papers or hear about on CNBC; nonetheless, they make up the bulk of new fund launches. The funds that launch with hundreds of millions or even billions of dollars are few and far between. If you are a manager who is launching with anywhere north of $500 million, first let me say thank you for buying my book, and second let me tell you to stop reading. With this sort of asset base, you don't need this book to help you. You probably could have written parts of it. You need only to manage the money successfully. I would go with a value approach and short good stories, but that is just me. You should stick with what you know, and again, thanks for buying the book.

Now back to reality. For those of you who will be operating in the real world, you need to be scrappy and willing to get dirt under your fingernails, because the opportunity is there. You just need to be able to see it and seize it. The plan, like most good things, will start at home.

The first place to begin is to examine your personal financial situation and get a complete picture of it. You need to be prepared to go without a salary for some time. You should have enough money in the bank to cover not only the lifestyle you and your family have become accustomed to, but also the immediate costs of launching the fund and managing the assets. One of the most important things that you need to do on your road to success is to make sure that all of your personal finances are in order so that you do not create undue stress at home. Taking care of this in the beginning will allow you to be more successful going forward and relieve one source of pressure in your life that can be quite burdensome when no money is coming in. Remember, being an entrepreneur is stressful enough, with all the nonsense and headaches that come from starting and running a business. The last thing you want to do is have stress at home. It is also important to make sure that your family and friends realize what you are doing. They don't necessarily have to be behind you and your new work, but it is important that they respect what you are trying to do. The frustration that comes from doing documents is enough to drive you crazy. It is important that the people around you know that your life has just hit stress factor nine and that you may need their support to deal with it.

If you are not used to working under self-imposed pressure or have a hard time dealing with the stress that comes naturally with being an entrepreneur, then I would suggest two things: (1) find a good business partner who will help you through the issues and problems that come up as the organization is formed and grows, and (2) find an activity that will allow you to burn the stress and relieve some of the pressure that will undoubtedly arise.

You should realize that all of the trials and tribulations that occur in your business have occurred in one way, shape, or form to other entrepreneurs and hedge fund managers. You are not alone in this. It is also important to realize that things do get better over time. If they don't, you will realize it and be smart enough to find a solution to make the situation better.

When it comes to making financial decisions, you need to have a sound mind. You need to make sure that you have enough money in the bank to avoid any financial pressures or stresses that can occur when you are not drawing a salary and have very little income. Most accountants and lawyers suggest having at least two years of living expenses in a money market or checking account that you can draw upon with ease as needed. You also need money to pay for service providers and infrastructure, a figure that can rise to at least $150,000. And you need to have at least $1 million in fund assets. It seems like a lot of money, and, quite frankly, it is, but by having these sorts of cushions, you will make your life a lot easier and keep things relatively normal until the business is up and running and generating fee income.

PRESSURES FROM TWO SIDES

Along with financial pressures, there are people pressures that go with launching a hedge fund. These pressures come from having to work closely with someone for the first time and learning how the person complements you and you complement him or her. Choosing a partner is very difficult and something that you should not take lightly. Hedge fund managers seem to pick friends or colleagues that they have some experience working with and with whom there is mutual admiration, trust, and respect. Finding a partner who is a friend is good, but it is also important to find someone or a couple of people who complement each other. The key here is to identify strengths and weaknesses and find people whose strengths are your weaknesses and whose weaknesses are your strengths.

What makes my firm successful is the preceding sentence. My partner and I complement each other almost perfectly. There is very little overlap, and that makes for a very easy and successful working relationship.

All partnerships endure stressful periods. There are many frustrations in the beginning and throughout a business, regardless of its size or shape. The key is to be able to work through the difficult times without having irreconcilable difficulties. In your business, think of your partner as your spouse. The key to making the relationship work is to have open and thoughtful communication during good times and bad. Without good, solid communication between the partners, the company will fail no matter how much money you get under management and how solid your track record becomes. Communication is the key to the success of the partnership. If you communicate, you will get along. Getting along is important because you will be spending a lot of time together, and there is nothing worse than spending time with people you don't like. As your business grows, so will the number of people in the organization. You may grow apart from your partner. Even if this does happen, you still need to be able to talk and to have the lines of communication open.

There is a long/short equity hedge fund with well over a billion dollars in assets under management. From the outside, it seems to be a very well run, successful organization. And indeed it is. In public, the partners seem to get along famously. They are jovial and really fun to be with. However, that is all a facade. When you go to their office and talk to them individually, you can see how much they truly detest each other and how difficult it is for them to work together each day. Their friendship has deteriorated, but their business partnership remains.

There have been times when I have spoken to one of the partners about something we are working on. Sometimes just two or three hours later, or even the next day, I will get a call from the other partner I did not talk to. He will ask me the same question and be looking for the same answers. At first I thought this was funny. Now I just find it sad. My initial thought was that the reason the two did not communicate was because they were so busy and did not have the time. However, I have come to find out that the reason they don't talk is because they can't stand being in the same room together. What makes the situation so interesting is that the partners have figured out how to make their lack of communication work and have built a successful business without liking each other. Even some of the employees don't realize that the two don't get along. One is responsible for the front office—trading and marketing—and the other is in charge of the back office, dealing with operations and customer relations. They interact on a day-to-day basis in a civil and professional manner.

"Look, you don't have to be best friends with your partners. You don't even need to see them outside of the office. All you have to do is be civil," said one of the partners, whom I will call Mike. "We don't get along anymore on a personal level, but I think that it is evident that the deterioration of our personal relationship has not affected our professional one, and investors do not need to worry because our performance is good and our operation runs smoothly."

The business has not suffered as a result of this strange, but probably somewhat normal, relationship. They are able to deal with issues that come up and work well under pressure to make sure the business does not suffer. They realize that they need each other for the greater good of the business and for each other's livelihood.

"We simply don't like each other anymore, but what are we going to do, split the business in two? That is just something we are not going to do, because it won't work for us," said the other partner, whom I will call Pete. "We both realize that no matter how bad it gets between us, at the end of the day we like what we do and know that we are better together than we would be apart."

A number of very successful hedge funds have been dissolved because the partners could not make it work anymore and believed that they would be better off on their own. In very few of these situations were the separated entities as successful on their own as they were when they were together. The lesson from these examples is to try to figure out a way to make it work, because the rewards are well worth it. You don't need to reinvent the wheel. You just need to make sure it keeps going round and round.

This situation with the preceding hedge fund partners is clearly an extreme one. In most partnerships, things do not get so bad that the partners can't stand each other. Nonetheless, you and your partner or partners should have clear definitions of each other's duties, understand each other's capabilities, and realize each other's strengths and weaknesses. This is how you will be successful even when things become difficult. In the beginning, it will help you get the firm up and running faster.

ROLE DEFINITION

Definition of duties is something that cannot be overlooked. More important is defining and agreeing on who will be the senior partner—the person who is ultimately responsible and who has the final say or vote over any and all decisions. This is one area of the start-up phase that often proves difficult. Yet you must check your ego at the door and work with your partner or partners to determine who will be the senior person. If you do not define this role, you will find it hard to get things done when times are tough, and decision making could become extremely difficult when the business is under stress. In the end, somebody has to have the final say or vote, and that person needs to know that the other partners will support his or her decision, no matter what it is. There needs to be a captain.

This person is not always the one with the most money invested in the fund or the business. It can be someone who has the best skill set and experience. It usually comes down to the partner with the most at risk. I have seen a number of organizations that ended up being run by someone who is clearly a junior financial partner but definitely the senior business partner. The choice needs to be made. It will be a hard one, but one that you have to make to really get things going.

The fund lawyers will give you some advice on how best to structure your partnership and will provide documents that govern the management of the partnership. You should also have these documents reviewed by your personal legal counsel, someone you trust and who works just for you. You should advise your partners to do the same. The person who reviews the partnership documents should not be connected to the business. Most likely, the fund counsel will not provide advice on these documents for individuals, since it would be a conflict. Therefore, get a fresh set of eyes to review the documents, one that is biased in favor of your and your family's needs. This person will make sure that your best interests are protected.

The partnership documents should address a number of serious issues, including, but not limited to, the death or disability of a partner and the compensation to the family if such a situation occurs. Everyone should be aware of what would happen to the partner's interest in the firm and how his or her family would be compensated should something happen. It will give all of you peace of mind and prevent the stress that accompanies these issues. Frequently, in the beginning, people choose not to deal with these issues because they feel that their business is not up and running or not successful yet and that the work is unnecessary. This is not true. Do not avoid dealing with it. Everything must be spelled out, and everyone must know where everyone else stands. Remember that you have responsibilities, so you need to be responsible.

Before you start dealing with the all the nitty-gritty of getting started, you need to sit down and determine how much capital you can commit to the fund for its operation and investment. You will put together a business plan that outlines the costs associated with launching and running the fund complex. You will try to put together an estimate of expected revenue. The revenue projections are quite simple if you use a simple management fee and incentive fee structure. Put all of this together to ensure you understand what you are committing yourself to financially and how much you may make when the venture is successful.

There are usually two or three ways to do things in life. When it comes to setting up a hedge fund, there are just two: (1) on your own and (2) as part of an institution. Since I believe that most people look to do it on their own, I will cover that first. If you are looking to build a fund within an existing platform of funds or through an institution, please skip the next few pages; the material you need begins later in this chapter.

You first need a timeline that details the various steps you must take to get your business off the ground. A number of prime brokers put out brochures and materials on how to get started. Most of that material is pretty good. All of the prime brokers say that one of the first things you need to do to get started is to pick your lawyer, your accountant, and your prime broker. If you are immediately building an offshore fund, you will also need to find an administrator. However, the law firm will provide you with advice on this, so you may be able to put it off for a few weeks.

The resource guide at the end of this book has a list of service providers to whom you will need to talk to get the business running. Most of the data in this chapter has been compiled from Web sites and publications deemed to be accurate; however, in some cases, particularly those of administrators, there may be inaccuracies or outdated information due to industry consolidation. Therefore, if you run into any problems finding specific service providers, please send me an e-mail at das@hedgeanswers.com and I will provide you with the most recent information I have. All of the service providers in this book will be happy to meet with you to discuss your situation and plans. I would suggest that you first meet with a number of lawyers. Three should be enough to start with. The reason for this number is that you want to be assured of the best execution and you want to make sure you are getting a good price. Remember, the hedge fund industry is a commodity business, and it should be treated as one when you are buying goods and services. This means that you should demand good service at reasonable prices. If that is not what the firm seems to be selling, move on to the next one.

GETTING GOING

As you start your process, I would try to meet with three lawyers and three or four prime brokers. Make sure they do what you do, meaning that if you are going to trade equities, then they should trade equities. Going to a fixed-income firm will waste your time and theirs. Meet with three accountants. You should be able to complete all of these meetings within the first week of your effort. At the end of the week, you should be able to determine who you want to see again, who you don't want to see, and who is in the running for your business. By the end of the second week, you should have this completed and be on your way.

When you meet with the lawyers, remember to ask them who is going to do the work, what it will cost, and when it will be completed. Most hedge fund lawyers are so experienced in preparing the documents that unless you are doing something completely different, the paperwork will be ready in 8 to 10 weeks. In terms of fees, you should expect to pay between $25,000 and $35,000 for the onshore fund and another $12,000 to $15,000 for the offshore fund. Some law firms charge less and some charge more. The key is to find a firm that you like, that you feel comfortable with, and that meets your budget requirements. You will also need to have accountants signed up almost immediately. While you probably will not work that closely with them in the beginning, you will need to have them review your documents prior to their being finalized. This should cost you less than $2,000. It is important and worth it.

As for the audit and tax fees, the current going rate for a big firm is about $35,000, while some smaller firms charge anywhere from $7,500 to $12,500. It is important that you keep this in perspective, because it is a significant cost, no matter what the size of the firm you choose. The audit in most cases is done at the completion of your first year in business. This means that if you start the fund in October 2006, you probably will not do an audit until January 2008. Most likely, it would not make sense to audit a three-month track record. So you would wait until you had a full year's performance under your belt. That means you will not have to pay the accountant for more than a year. However, if you start in May 2007, you most likely will do the audit in January 2008. This means that you will have to pay the accountant within seven months of opening your doors. This may mean that you have to use a significant portion of your start-up capital to cover the expense. In light of the new regulations regarding registration, there may be new rules pertaining to when a fund is audited. Your fund counsel will give you the most up-to-date information on this issue.

Once you figure out who your lawyer, accountant, and prime broker are going to be, the next thing you need to do is to look for office space and start thinking about human and nonhuman infrastructure. Office space is important because it will provide a clear and defined base for your operation. You will also need to determine how many people you will need to get the business up and running—whether you should hire people right out of the gate or wait until assets and fees come through the door.

In my opinion, if you are starting with less than $100 million in assets under management, it is probably best if you and your partner or partners do most of the work yourselves to keep costs low and in check. If you are gong it alone, however, you should hire someone to help you. This person will become a solid member of your team and will make the process run a lot smoother.

Most of the things that you need to do to get set up are relatively easy but tedious. You should know how things work so that if there are problems, you know how to deal with them. Use the guideline in the back of this book to help you identify items that need to be addressed. It will help you figure out the steps you need to complete the launch sequence and have all systems go.

If there are more than two partners, you most likely will not need to hire anyone, except to satisfy your egos. If you think any job in your operation is beneath you or are embarrassed to perform any task related to your business, you are destined to fail. A lot of people starting out come from organizations with a big infrastructure and huge resources and don't have to work so hard on the things that make the business run. As an entrepreneur, this is just not the case. You need to be in charge at all times. If you are not prepared to do that, then I suggest that you not leave your current position.

One of the first jobs to fill is that of facilities manager. In this capacity, you will be in charge of finding office space and outfitting it with all the tools you need to be successful. There are two schools of thought in dealing with office space in the hedge fund world: The first is to take advantage of what the prime brokers offer in their hedge fund hotels, and the other is to go out and find your own space. Cost and time should not be the deciding factors. You should create an environment in which you will thrive. If you are used to working in a big space with lots of people to talk to and exchange ideas with, then it might make sense to work out of one of the hotels or perhaps sublet space from another fund or money management firm. If this is something that does not appeal to you, and you work better on your own without distractions or other people around, then getting your own space is probably the best thing for you to do.

Ultimately, you should choose a place you believe will provide the most comfortable work environment for you and where you think you will be able to thrive. You should not make a decision based solely on the cost of the setup.

Most likely, you will save money by working out of a hedge fund hotel because of the scale of these operations. The prime brokers are buying everything in bulk and generally pass the savings along to the managers in their space. But remember that everything comes with a price. If you are in a prime broker's hotel, then you are going to have to trade with those people, borrow securities from them for your shorts, and pay them rent. You may be free to trade with whomever you want, but you will also be expected to put business through their desks.

The one thing about going with a hotel is that it will probably save an enormous amount of time and the frustration that goes along with outfitting any piece of real estate. This alone makes hotels look pretty attractive. In the hotels, everything you need is at your fingertips. For the most part, the facilities are very nice, clean, and up-to-date. They offer you the ability to be up and running in a day or two. If you do it yourself, setting up the infrastructure will take significantly longer and be a lot more work. It will also be more expensive in the short run because you will have to lay out working capital to cover the costs of computers, furniture, and other things you need to complete the space.

Either way is fine. In the end, it will come down to weighing the benefits of going with space that your prime broker has available versus going out on your own. You will need to see which makes the most business and economic sense for your operation. Then choose one and go with it.

STUFF TO DO

The problem with being an entrepreneur is that there are a lot of decisions that need to be made and executed that relate to the business, but that don't necessarily relate to the money management side of the business. You will need to figure out insurance, rent, lights, phone, technology, furniture, business cards, stationery, and even coffee. These can be daunting tasks for even the most qualified executives.

As an employee, you are used to having someone else do all of this for you, which provides you with the freedom to simply go about your business. Now the business of the business is part of your job. It is not always easy to juggle both. I think that one of the best decisions a new fund manager can make is to find a partner who is a good, solid office manager, someone who has experience working with you, who knows your style, and who will fit into the new culture that you are developing. The key to this hire is that the person is going to be given a lot of responsibility right out of the gate. You must have a firm grasp of his or her abilities. More important, you must have faith and trust that your partner will execute appropriately on your behalf and make good decisions that you do not have to double-check.

Over the years, a number of managers I have talked to about how they got started in the business have said that the biggest mistake they made from the outset was trying to do everything themselves. They all generally agreed that what they are good at is making money in the markets and what they are not good at is the logistics of running an office. This led them to realize that they needed someone to step in and fill this gap. The solution was a good administrative assistant.

"Our fund started off pretty small, and so we thought the right thing was to stay small in terms of staff. What we did not realize was all the time it took to get the everyday aspects of the business up and running smoothly," said a fund manager. "We spent as much if not more time working on getting our business up and running smoothly than we did managing the little money we had and prospecting for new investors in the first six months. It was a mistake. We should have hired someone to handle all that stuff for us so we could focus on managing money."

There are clearly a lot of hassles and distractions that go along with setting up your physical plant. In the beginning, it will look as though the pros outnumber the cons. But you need to go with your gut on this.

Our firm has gone through both. Having our own office—even though it was an absolute nightmare to complete the renovations and get set up— ended up providing us with a nicer and more functional space than the one we previously had in a hotel complex. We decided to go with a hotel to save time and money, and we used it as a stopgap position.

Whatever you choose to do will be fine. You can always choose to move. Irrespective of your office arrangement, you must pay close attention to your service providers. In this case, I mean the phone company, Internet service provider, and computer support staff. You need to make sure that they can provide you with everything you need to get your business operational in a reasonable time frame. Make them give you a schedule and force them to stick to it. There is nothing more frustrating than wanting to do something and not being able to do it because a service provider is not ready. It is also important that you make sure you know whom to call if you have a problem and need to get something fixed. Remember the Nancy Havens story!

As an entrepreneur, you must realize that you will be on the bottom of the list in almost everything you do in the beginning, because there will always be someone bigger than you who needs help at the same time. It will be humbling at first, but the rewards that come with running your own shop will make it all worthwhile. You will get the service you need, but you will get it when the service provider wants to give it to you.

Most prime brokers offer help in this area to make the transition smoother. Yet it will be difficult and will take some getting used to. Regarding service providers, make sure of two things: (1) Pay your bills on time, and (2) deal with them directly. Regardless of what they do, people should be treated with respect. The old adage that you catch more flies with honey than with vinegar is very true.

If you treat service providers the way you want them to treat you, then you have a relationship that is mutually beneficial. Don't be demanding and overbearing. They won't like it and won't want to service you. This means you will be down for the count until you find someone else to fix the problem. The last thing in the world that you want to have happen is to lose a trade or go without needed research because you irritated the tech support personnel in the office. This is not what you should be worrying about as you build your business.

All of these issues fade away if you decide that you want to build your hedge fund inside an existing organization. Fortunately for you, there are a number of ways to do this, and this is an area of the industry that is gaining significantly in popularity.

MULTISTRATEGY FUND

One type of organization that is offering platforms for new managers is the multistrategy hedge fund firm. These fund complexes usually consist of a slew of traders who trade various strategies and instruments under a single umbrella organization. In most cases, the firm uses a risk model to determine its tolerance for various strategies and dials up its allocation of assets accordingly. If you work in this type of environment, you are really being a prop trader for a hedge fund, although some fund groups allow traders to set up their own structures. This allows them to accept money from the outside along with the fund complex. Consequently, you are not really going out on your own.

Another opportunity that exists for hedge fund managers is to work within an organizational structure that I call a "proprietary" fund of funds. In this situation, you as the manager agree to trade for the firm. In turn, the firm goes out and raises assets for you and runs all of the administrative aspects of the operation. Together you split the fees; in most cases, it is 70 percent for you and 30 percent for the firm. There are situations in which the fee split is more in your favor. I would try for an 80/20 split, but it never should be lower than 70/30. Most firms like doing this because it keeps their costs lower and allows them to offer multiple products to potential investors with little or no additional effort. Fund complexes usually will market you in two ways: as a part of their fund of funds or multistrategy fund or as a stand-alone fund. In either case, all you do is trade the money and collect your fees. It can be quite rewarding for both you and the fund you are working with.

The third option is to go to a trading house that offers seeding platforms for hedge funds. In the wake of the bursting of the technology bubble, a number of former day-trading shops have reinvented themselves as independent trading platforms. Some of these shops exist in Manhattan and operate in a way similar to the old day-trading shops when the Nasdaq was roaring. They provide some seed capital and allow you to build a business using their trading platform. You will work out of their offices, share ideas with their proprietary traders, and use them for the bulk of your order executions. In some cases, managers are asked to manage firm capital along with their fund assets. This can provide for a nice additional income stream. Operating out of one of these trading houses is similar to working out of a hedge fund hotel. However, you do give up some autonomy.

Another option that many people are using to get their businesses off the ground is to work with a seeding company. These have been around for quite some time. They offer start-up funds access to pools of capital. In most cases, the seeder will take a piece of the equity in your firm and will need to be guaranteed a certain level of capacity in the fund as it grows. These companies work with funds across all strategies and provide capital ranging in size from $1 million to $50 million. Over the past year or so, becoming a seeder has developed into a very popular business. There are cases in which insurance companies, large hedge funds, large money management firms, and even an endowment have decided to get into the business of seeding managers. It is a growing trend in the industry and one that is probably a good solution for most new managers looking for capital to grow their businesses.

If you are interested in learning more about seeders or the other platforms discussed in this chapter, you are welcome to e-mail me with your questions at the address listed previously. I will provide you with information on various organizations willing to work with these types of transactions and structures and give you answers to any specific questions that you have about this aspect of the industry.

This chapter should have provided you with the insight and guidelines you need to get started on your journey in the hedge fund business. Unfortunately, there will be a lot of questions that come up before, during, and after the process of getting you into the hedge fund business begins. You will need to find good resources to provide you with answers. In my experience, the person who has given me the best answers from a business perspective has always been my firm's accountant. Regardless of the issue or question, he always seems to be able to give me good, solid, tactical advice and provide me with the resources to make the best decision. Unfortunately, most lawyers are not businesspeople and thus usually are not good at providing advice about the business side of your enterprise. However, they will always keep you out of trouble and tell you when you are doing something wrong. Use both relationships wisely and you will find most of your answers. The rest you can make up as you go along. It is the only way you are truly going to learn the business.

CHAPTER 9

Perception versus Reality

Today is the first day of the rest of your life. Now what?

That is what you will think as soon as you decide to get into the hedge fund business. It is both frightening and exhilarating. This is it. You are moving forward. You are about to take a wild and exciting ride, and you are either going to rocket to the moon or crash-land in the desert. You are now one of the few and the proud—a person who chases dreams, an entrepreneur. All that is left is to build a successful business.

As you step out of the corporate world, you need to make sure you have a positive attitude and stay focused on the tasks at hand. It is important to feel good about your decision and be proud that you took the plunge, but remember that feeling good and being proud are not going to pay the bills or build your business. You need to pay attention, get things moving, and begin putting in place a plan that will provide you with success and, more important, an answer to the question, "Now what?"

In the hedge fund business, every day is the first day of the rest of your life. Performance is bad? Don't worry. You can make it up tomorrow. Cannot raise any assets? You will find a way to do it tomorrow or the next. If you get that through your head, you will be able to be successful. Don't get discouraged, because being discouraged leads to a lack of enthusiasm. A lack of enthusiasm can lead to depression. And that can lead to failure!

DAY 1

The first thing you need to do is ensure that you don't buy into the theory that if you build it, they will come. This works only in the movies. Read the sentence 25 more times, and don't forget it. When push comes to shove, the only way you will be successful in this business is by working hard and going after it. Waiting for people to come to you will lead to failure. Hoping and expecting is for fools. If you don't believe the previous sentence, stop reading this book and go directly to the classifieds. You need to find a job.

Remember, however, that hard work does not guarantee success. It doesn't necessarily mean failure, either. It just means that you are a hard worker. The key to success is to work hard and to work smart. By working hard and working smart, you will not fail.

Frequently, when people enter the hedge fund business, they think about several things that cause them to lose sight of what it is important. They think about how much money they are going to make, what kind of yacht they are going to sail, how big a house they are going to move into, what kind of art collection they are going to acquire, how much money they can give to charity so that others can see how successful they have become, and what kind of cars they are going to own. Thinking about these things will lead to failure. Instead, you need to focus on three issues: raising assets, managing assets, and operating the business successfully. You need to make sure you have the staff, systems, and infrastructure in place to make the machine run smoothly and efficiently. Forget about the luxuries. These will come with time. Instead, concentrate on building a successful business and what you need to do to make this a reality.

Hal Holbrook, who played Lou Mannheim in Oliver Stone's film *Wall Street*, said to young Bud Fox, played by Charlie Sheen, after receiving an inside tip: "Quick buck artists come and go with every bull market. The steady players make it through the bear market.[1]

This is what you want to do. You want to be a steady player who builds something that lasts. There is no need to waste time on things that don't matter. Instead, stay focused on the business at hand, which is building your firm. Most people who start off building a business do not set out thinking that they are going to become extremely rich from their endeavor. Most start off thinking that this is something that they are good at, that they can do successfully, and that will allow them to do what they want to do with their time.

If you were to ask Ray Kroc, Warren Buffett, or anyone else we equate with extreme success, about their thoughts on being an entrepreneur, I believe they would say that they did not start out to revolutionize the way people go to restaurants or set the benchmark for investors all over the world. Rather, I believe they would say that they had an idea, believed in themselves, and went forward with it. That is exactly what you are going to have to do as a hedge fund manager.

My recipe for successful hedge fund management—besides assets, strong asset management skills, and a solid infrastructure—includes the following: (1) Stick with what you know, (2) adapt to change, and (3) listen to ideas. You also need to make sure you do *not* check your ego at the door. You are the same as nearly 10,000 people selling basically the same product to the same people, except for one thing—you are better than all of them! You are faster, better, and smarter than everyone else, and you want the world to know it. In this business, being an egomaniac is a good thing.

EGOS MATTER

Hedge fund managers who do not check their egos at the door are the ones who are successful and the ones who come out on top! The ones who do check their egos at the door are the ones who are not successful and end up waiting for something to happen. Remember: A watched pot never boils. This is kill or be killed. The question is, are you ready for combat?

I know that there are some people sitting at home reading this saying that this can't be true and this is not the way it works. Let me tell you something: Ask any hedge fund managers you know whether they consider themselves the best around. The ones who say no are the ones you don't want to invest with or emulate. The ones who say yes are the ones you want to invest with and learn from.

It is counterintuitive to the way we were taught the world works. This is why some hedge fund managers fail and others succeed. If managers have egos or a chip on their shoulder, it is going to be hard for them to see the truth or see what is really going on. To some, that may be a problem. But in reality, it is exactly the way you need to be when you are in the marketplace looking for assets and managing money!

- You need to believe that you are the best money manager in the world.
- You need to believe that you can pick the winners and losers before everybody else.
- You need to believe that you understand the yield curve better than everyone else and that you understand the value of buying something cheap and watching it become expensive.
- You have to think in your heart of hearts that you are the best and that you should be in the hall of fame, along with all the other great managers.

If you do not believe that you have built a better mousetrap or figured out a better way to skin a cat, then you are going to fail. The whole idea of this book is to get you to understand the steps and tools you need to be successful in the hedge fund business. The last few chapters are about what I call the bricks-and-mortar side of the business. This chapter is about the mental side of it. It should help you understand how to be successful, where success comes from, and how it can be used to truly make you a winner.

In the hedge fund business, success comes down to one thing: your ability to communicate to investors and potential investors that you have an extraordinary ability to find opportunities in the market and make money from them. This is the crux of everything that you will do from now on; it is the thesis of offering documents; it is the backbone of your marketing presentations; it is the thread that runs through every conversation you will have from this day forward. It is all about exploiting the markets and your ability to create profits from these opportunities. The question you need to answer is, do you have it in you?

The answer is yes. How do I come to this conclusion? It is simple. If you didn't, you would not be reading this book. By buying the book, you have demonstrated that you have at least the fundamental requirement for successful entrepreneurship—curiosity. The road ahead is going to be tough, but you will be able to travel it.

THE ACTION PLAN

The first thing you need is an action plan. This will provide you with a road map for your business. The map must not be written in stone. Rather, it should be a fluid, movable document that allows you to see where you are going and prepare you to get there. Completing the journey should take about 12 weeks. That is the time needed to get the fund up and running after your initial conversation with your lawyer. It is important to set a reasonable time frame and make sure you stay on track. The map should keep you focused on the task at hand and guide you through the process. As part of their welcome package, some prime brokers provide timelines and guidance on getting started. These materials will prove useful and effective as you launch the fund.

I think the best place to start is to first decide what your capital needs are and where the funds will come from. Unless you make a seeding deal right out of the box, you and your partners will have to front all of the money. This is actually a good way to ensure that everyone is honest and motivated. However, this could put a serious financial drain on you and your partners, and you might want to assess all of your individual needs, expectations, and wants to make sure you do not get stuck before you've started. If you don't have the financial wherewithal to get the fund up and running, it is a mistake to get started in the first place. You need to make sure you not only have enough money to launch the fund, but also that you and your partners have money in the bank to cover living expenses for at least the first year or so.

Once you decide on capital, the next thing to do is to pick a lawyer, an accountant, and a prime broker. Each will provide you with insight on various aspects of the industry that will be both good and bad—most of it good—and will give you the tools to get the infrastructure of the business up and running. During the interview stage, it is important to talk to everyone you know about the industry and running a fund. Also, you need to stay focused on putting together investor lists with up-to-date contact details so that when you launch the fund you have some assets to manage.

The key here is to stay focused, use the time to plan, and act according to your map. During the prelaunch and launch phases, many new managers lose sight of the investor. There is nothing more important than having a list of potential investors ready to go and in the queue. Then when you come out of the gate, you will have people to talk to and, more important, some money to manage. It is very important to put a lot of effort into investor lists and marketing from the beginning of the process. It is never too early to start working on this area of your business. You will not regret it.

The way for me to illustrate this and other points relating to the fund's start-up and launch is by providing three case studies on hedge funds—one that failed and two that succeeded. In each of the case studies, the principals started with the best of intentions. They all knew how to trade markets. They all knew how to make money. And they all believed they knew what to do to be successful. However, as we shall learn in the pages that follow, each of them attacked the problems of raising assets and building a business differently. One decided to build a business in his home with a childhood friend. One decided to build a business with a partner who acted as financial backer. And the third took his own personal wealth, which he accumulated in a successful run on Wall Street, built a small fund on his own, and then found a seed partner.

Case Study 1: The Manager Who Did Not Make It!

The first story begins in a small town about 30 miles south of Boston, with a manager who had been trading stocks for a number of large Wall Street brokerage firms. He built a fine reputation for himself on the Street. Over time, he developed a successful methodology for navigating the markets on a daily basis, using both his own capital and the firm's. Over time, he made a significant amount of money for his firm and himself. After a few years, he decided to take his experience and put it to work in a hedge fund.

The manager, whom I will call Tom, partnered with a friend of his from high school—whom I will call Charlie. Tom believed Charlie would be a good CEO or CFO, someone who could help him build and run the business side of things. This would allow Tom to stay focused on trading stocks and managing the portfolio. Tom also decided that, instead of commuting every day into downtown Boston, he would take a spare room in his house and turn it into his office. The rationale was that it was cheaper, better, and more efficient to build the infrastructure in his house than it would be to rent space and start from scratch. After a while, he built an addition onto the side of the house by closing in a deck. The operation looked as good as that of other start-up managers. It had phones, faxes, computers, a Bloomberg— basically everything at his fingertips needed to trade and manage money. It also offered Tom the ability to roll out of bed and be in the office and at his desk in a matter of minutes.

Having the office in his house proved to be both a blessing and a curse. It was a blessing because he was able to spend time with his family and live a simple, peaceful life. It was a curse because investors generally did not take him or his operation seriously. Working out of his home became a hindrance to raising capital.

Tom started with $1.5 million of his own money and immediately attracted a few investors who were friends and family. Charlie put in about a million dollars of his money. By the time the fund was launched in January 2000, it had approximately $3 million in assets under management. From the outset, the partners used well-respected and well-regarded service providers, including Goldman as their prime broker, GGK as their auditor, and Rosenman and Collin as their law firm. Regardless of market perception, the business was a serious concern, and as a reflection of this, used serious service providers.

During the first six months of 2000, the fund did extremely well. The portfolio weathered the bursting of the technology bubble and finished the year with strong numbers. In 2001, Tom also managed the portfolio quite well and again finished the year strong. Unfortunately, during this time, he attracted few assets. A number of funds of funds and other investors seemed to like what he was saying, what he was doing, and how he performed, yet when the investors did due diligence, they could not overcome the hurdle of Tom working out of his home. They simply did not respect him or his operation. They felt that he was not serious about building a business, so they always passed on investing in the fund.

Tom's initial reaction was that once people saw his track record, they would get over the hurdle of the home office and be convinced. Unfortunately, this was not the case.

"I thought people would see the track record and see that the fund was growing, and one thing will lead to another and the money will come in based on our performance," he said. "This was not the case. I kept hoping that the perception would change and that people would forget about the office and focus on the track record."

After three years, he decided to call it quits. During this time he was able to raise only an additional $2 or $3 million. This was not enough to support the business or his family.

The problem was that Tom wanted to have his cake and eat it, too. He enjoyed working out of his home. He enjoyed the fact that he could see his children off to school and greet them when they came home at night. He enjoyed the fact that he was able to go to his son's baseball games in the spring and summer and to another son's soccer practice and games in the fall. Tom enjoyed the fact that he was able to participate in his children's lives. He enjoyed the fact that he could have dinner with his family, help his kids with their homework, put them to bed, perhaps watch some television with his wife, and then go back into the home office for a few hours and have everything that he needed at his fingertips. He enjoyed the operation that he had built and he enjoyed the lifestyle he was leading. The only problem: He couldn't raise money.

The other problem was that he put too much trust and responsibility in Charlie. Unfortunately for Tom, Charlie had little experience running a business, managing assets, or building an operation. What he did have was experience as an order clerk, a position he had held at a large institutional brokerage firm. Charlie knew how to traffic trades, check out at the end of the day, and make sure that trades were being properly credited and correctly accounted for. However, what he did not know was how to deal with infrastructure issues—the heart and soul of the hedge fund business and the core that everything is built around. A business needs to find someone to deal with these things on a day-to-day, minute-by-minute basis. Charlie was not this guy. Needless to say, Tom became extremely frustrated with the operation and with his friend.

However, his frustration existed on a number of different levels. He was frustrated that he had traded the markets successfully during one of its most volatile periods, yet no one seemed to care. He was frustrated that he could not raise assets despite having contacts on and around the Street. And he was frustrated because the person he expected to be able to create, deliver, and run the infrastructure and build a business was failing and incapable of doing what needed to be done.

After three years of frustration, he began to question what to do and how to deal with it. Unfortunately, his decision was that it was not worth it to run the business any longer, that it was better for him to call it a day. The problem was that he could not just fold up the tent and go home. After coming to the conclusion that he needed to shut down, he worked for about another year to wind down the business and close up shop.

When he gave back the assets that he had received from investors, he was able to do so with pride. All of them had made money with him. During his tenure as a stand-alone manager, he put up good, solid numbers and made money for his partners. He built it, but unfortunately no one came.

Looking back on his experience, Tom told me that his real problem was not that he had an office in his house, but rather that he did not have a seed investor to give him critical mass. "If I had gotten someone with $10 or $20 million, other investors would not have cared about where I was running the firm," he said. "They would have seen that I had real money and would have been interested in investing. The location of the office would not have been an issue."

Along with not finding a seed investor, another error that he made was that he hired a friend. In fact, he calls it the biggest mistake of his life. "In retrospect, hiring Charlie really made no sense at all. I should have seen that going in, and I just missed it completely," he said. "It would have been better to hire someone who I did not know very well and, more importantly, someone with the experience I needed, rather than relying on a person who I thought it would have been fun to work with."

In terms of running the fund from his house, he does not believe that this was an error. He actually thinks that it was great, and he believes that it allowed him to maintain a quality of life that extremely few Wall Street and hedge fund people enjoy.

Unfortunately, today he works for a large brokerage firm in Boston, traveling back and forth by train every day to the city. As a consequence, he has been unable to maintain that quality of life. He says that he has very few regrets about not being able to run his business or build it into the type of organization that he wanted to. He maintains that shutting it down was the right thing to do. He thought that there was too much stress being put on him as an entrepreneur and that it would eventually affect his performance.

"I did the right thing by my investors, and that is all that matters," he said. "Having learned from my mistakes will let me be more successful and help me get back on track when the time is right. Someday, I will be running a fund again. It will take some time, but this time it will last a lot longer."

Case Study 2: Two Guys in Search of a Third!

This is the story of two individuals—a marketing guy and an investment guy. The marketing guy knows next to nothing about managing money, and the investment guy knows little about raising money. So they make a great pair.

The two worked in a large institutional brokerage firm for a number of years and in this capacity they became friends. The marketing guy had previously worked at a number of the big brokerage firms and had developed incredibly deep and solid relationships with people at those firms at the highest of levels of the organization. The money manager was previously at a large endowment, managing assets for them after starting his career working at the Treasury Department. In his early days, he spent a lot of time doing economic research and learning about interest rates, money supply, and the markets. When he went to the large endowment, he was given its fixed-income portfolio and managed that for a number of years. He later took a position at the brokerage firm running company and client assets. Through one of Wall Street's twists of fate, the two gentlemen landed at the brokerage firm and became fast friends. A few years into their working together, the firm was sold to a large domestic bank, and they were both forced to leave the company. They decided that their next move was going to be one in which they could not get fired! They decided to set up a hedge fund.

They understood that both of them had not yet made it on Wall Street—meaning that they had not yet amassed millions of dollars to launch a fund, nor had they amassed the financial wherewithal that they thought they needed to run a business. As a result, they needed a money partner. They decided to harness some of the relationships that the marketing guy had with people looking for the chance to be entrepreneurs. They wanted to turn those relationships into a seeding opportunity.

These two gentlemen put together a business plan that detailed the opportunity in the marketplace, the upside for investors, and the upside for them. The plan included hypothetical examples of the strategy and provided simulated performance data. They used the document to go into the market with a clear and concise message and objectives. Through their relationships, they were able to find a small family office in the Los Angeles area that was willing to become a partner with them and provide them with financial backing. The team now consisted of the marketing guy, the money manager, and the family office that was going to provide working capital and infrastructure support. Together, the team would develop a business, and within a few months, the three partners launched their hedge fund.

One of the first things they did when they launched the business was to get the strategy up and running immediately. They started with about $5 million, primarily from the three partners and some outsiders, and they began trading from the first day.

"We thought it was important to get things going," said the money manager. "We did not want to wait, so we opened an account and started trading from day one. If we had a dollar we would have started. The assets didn't matter. What we wanted was to build a track record."

By having the family office involved, the marketer and the money manager were able to concentrate on their specific duties and let their other partner take care of the business operation. The working capital that the family provided was used to pay the lawyers, the accountants, and other start-up costs associated with the fund's launch. More important, the family also provided the team with ongoing working capital that was used to maintain the firm and its infrastructure, as well as to provide salaries while the fund was establishing itself.

Together, the three operated in sync. Each paid attention to his specific duties and focused on the tasks at hand to get things up and running.

In the beginning, it was very difficult to raise money. A number of people, specifically institutional investors, believed that the marketing person and the family office had little or no interest in the hedge fund business and that they had too many outside interests distracting them from spending time with the fund.

"People questioned our commitment," said the marketer. "It was very frustrating. We would go to meetings, explain the strategy, show them the track record and the hypotheticals. They would get excited, and then all of the sudden, they started questioning whether we were serious, and we would spend the next half hour trying to convince them that we were focused on the fund and that we put our other interests aside."

However, as time progressed, the track record grew and in the second year, the fund started attracting assets. The numbers drove investors to the fund. The fund went from having about $5 million the first year to around $50 million by the end of the second. Since then, things have progressed quite nicely. Over the past two-and-a-half years, the firm has grown to about $350 million in assets under management. The reason for the partners' success is threefold:

1. The day-to-day responsibilities at the organization were clearly defined.
2. They had the financial wherewithal to meet all of their financial commitments without placing any stress on the business or the individuals.
3. They were consistent with their investment strategy.

By staying focused, being consistent, and having the money to weather the storms, the partners have become successful entrepreneurs and, more important, successful hedge fund managers. "We have been able to create a business base by paying attention to these three things," said the money manager. "More importantly, we stuck with our plan and we did what we set out to do."

These people attacked the business no differently than you would attack any other type of business. They did not wait for things to happen, they made things happen, and it worked for them.

"We defined our responsibilities. We put together a real budget that had real numbers and put a plan together that would allow us to truly be successful," the marketer said. "Not only did we do it when we first started out but continue to do it today. We have added staff, and in turn spread out some of the responsibilities. But in the end, we all know where we stand and what we are working for and truly have our eye on the prize."

I expect that by the end of 2006, the fund will have more than $500 million in assets. The fund's track record is good, the management is stable, the strategy is easy to understand, and frankly, the whole thing makes sense. Over the past few years, the partners have hired additional staff to help them manage and run the business more efficiently. They have added a chief operating officer, who deals with all client relations and all operational aspects of the business. They have added an analyst, who helps the money manager with the investment strategy, and they have added an office assistant, who handles all of the firm's administrative functions. The team now totals six. It is a successful business and it is something that their investors and potential investors seem to really appreciate and respect. Hedge fund investors are looking for funds that have a strong, well-thought-out organization and that offer good, solid numbers regardless of market conditions. When investors look at this fund, that is exactly what they see. It is because of this that the fund is attracting assets at such a fast pace and that it is able to expand so quickly.

Case Study 3: The Manager and the Seeder

This is the story of a well-respected, well-received, very smart investor who spent the first 10 years of his career after graduating from Harvard Business School managing money for other people. He helped many money managers earn a lot of money and finally decided that it was time to go out on his own. When he did, he hired a good lawyer. He engaged a good prime broker. He retained a well-known hedge fund accounting firm. And he hired a good administrator. He took these four service providers and opened a small office in midtown Manhattan, and presto, his fund was in business.

Unfortunately, throughout his first year of operation, he did not gather any assets or gain any traction. Frankly, he was stuck in a rut. There was clearly more to the story of the fund than just one guy in a room in Manhattan. He could not find anyone interested in learning about what he was doing or how he was doing it. When we met in early January 2006 to reminisce about his launch, he told me that it had been a bit depressing, unsettling, and really frustrating.

"It was quite apparent early on that I did not know the first thing about raising assets and how to actually run the business of a hedge fund, " said the manager, whom I will call Mike. "After a while, I realized that I had committed to the business, made the investment in the fund, and decided to gather as much as I could from friends and family, and then spend the rest of the time building a track record, which I thought I would be able to market and use to gather assets."

The first thing Mike did was to hire an analyst, a former colleague with whom he had managed money before and who understood his investment philosophy and strategy. Instead of hiring the person as an employee, however, he decided to make him a junior partner. After meeting with Mike, the analyst/partner realized immediately that they needed to make sure the fund had good numbers. He also realized that he would be responsible for doing the research and finding new ideas, as well as paying attention to many of the day-to-day details of running a fund. The key to Mike's strategy was good research and follow-through with the companies that they targeted for the portfolio.

"We work very hard looking for nuggets of information that we can turn into ideas," said Eric, who is Mike's partner. "My job is to not only assist Mike with what he is working on but to also work independently to find ideas that we can put into the portfolio. In the beginning, I was also the chief cook and bottle washer, meaning that I was responsible for a lot of the daily things that make the business run."

Mike believed that if the numbers were strong, the assets would come. "The only way people care about you is if you are able to put up good numbers," he said. "So we work really hard at putting up good numbers. It may sound silly but I think a lot of people are happy with mediocre numbers. That doesn't work for us."

The two spend a lot of time developing a portfolio that performs well, regardless of the way the market moves. They try to buy businesses that are cheap and to short businesses that are frauds. That is their story, and it's what they do to make the portfolio work for them. Throughout the first year of operation, the fund did very well. The two put up good, solid numbers, and people began to take notice.

In the second year, they discovered that numbers were not driving assets and found it very, very difficult to raise money. Mike decided to go after alumni from his days at Harvard Business School. He talked to as many people as he could and tried to find people to invest in the fund. He also expanded his network to find a seeding partner.

"We talked to so many different people—famous money managers, not famous money managers, respected money managers, disrespected money managers—all around the country, all around the world, the conversations were really endless," he said. We met with people looking to be seed partners, and finally we made a deal with a group that most people would never have thought would seed a start-up fund."

Mike found an extremely well-respected, large hedge fund to put up $5 million, with an additional commitment of $15 million if he proved himself. The hedge fund was looking to expand its research and analytical tools and realized that by seeding this de novo hedge fund, it would have access not only to new money management talent, but also to Mike's ideas, which had the potential to become part of the firm's own portfolio.

"They bought into us because they believed that not only would we do good things with their money, but that we would also provide them with ideas for their portfolio," Mike said. "It turned out to be a win-win for both of us. We get a well-heeled investor who made a substantial financial commitment to help us build the business, and they get an outlet for ideas that can help them with their portfolio."

Initially, this seeder came up with $5 million, and the fund jumped from about $1.5 million to $6.5 million in a very short period of time. The initial $5 million was a test, and once Mike and Eric proved themselves, the seeder gave them an additional $15 million, and the fund's assets crossed the $25 million mark. At $25 million, the fund started sparking the interest of potential investors, who saw that the numbers were strong and that the fund was delivering on its strategy. Slowly but surely, assets began to come in. Within five years, the fund went from $1 million to more than $100 million.

"All we have done is to deliver on what we said we were going to do, which was to employ a deep value, long/short strategy that shorts frauds (companies that are fraudulent)," said Mike. "Benjamin Graham, Warren Buffett, and Scott Black—we took all the things that these guys have proved to work, regardless of market conditions, and we do the same thing on a day-to-day basis."

Mike and Eric built a very good business based on sticking to what they knew worked. They realized it was going to be difficult. They realized the only way they could build their business was to build it alongside someone else. Thankfully, they found a good seeding partner who was able to kick-start their organization and set it on the right track.

As a fund manager, your job is to determine what is going to allow you to build a successful business. The only way you can do that is through the development and implementation of a reasonable and solid business plan. The plan should allow you to build a business that will stand the test of time and the markets and that will allow you to make money for your investors, you, your partners, and the people who work for you. That is your job.

I hope that in the last few chapters you have learned what you need to do to get started, launch your fund, and run your business. I set out to teach you what you need to do to build a fund, to identify markets that assets will come from, and to make decisions about how to build your business. That has been the goal of this book. If you have any questions about what you have read, feel free to e-mail me at das@hedgeanswers.com. I would be happy to answer any and all of your questions.

The future is very bright for the hedge fund industry because many smart people have realized that the only way to really make money in the market is to have tools available to investors as arrows in their quivers. The only way to do that is to be able to go long and short with the market. Hedge funds provide the managers with the necessary structure to perform, regardless of market conditions. And investors need to have good numbers regardless of whether the market rises or falls. Hedge funds are the only way to achieve these goals. You have realized that the future is about being able to go long and short with the market. That is the journey you are embarking on, and it is the journey that will bring you success as you build a thoughtful and well-run organization.

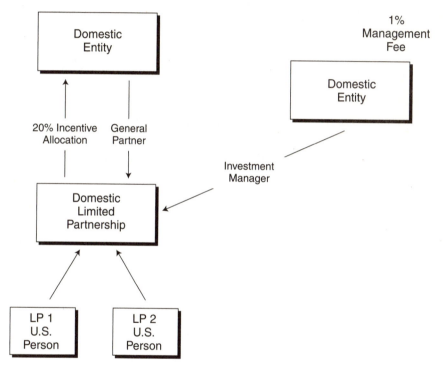

FIGURE A.1 Simple Onshore Structure
Source: Created and reprinted by permission of Maury Cartine, JD, CPA.

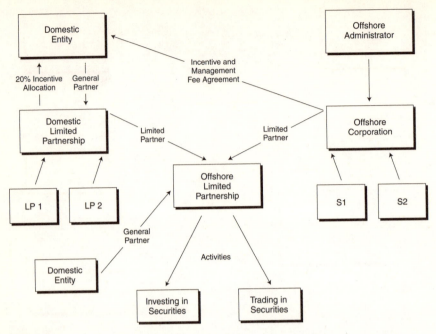

FIGURE A.2   Classic Master-Feeder Structure
Source: Created and reprinted by permission of Maury Cartine, JD, CPA.

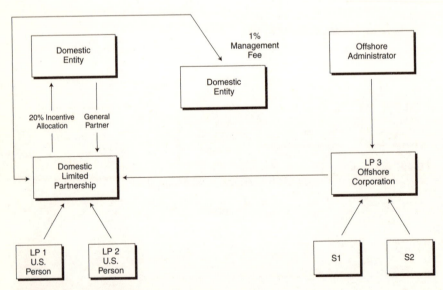

FIGURE A.3   Modified Master-Feeder Structure
Source: Created and reprinted by permission of Maury Cartine, JD, CPA.

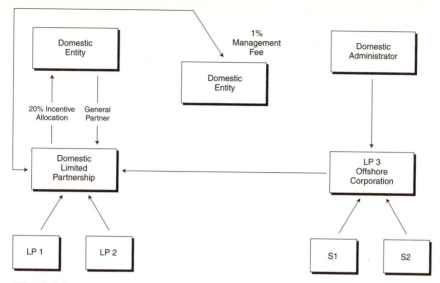

FIGURE A.4 Modified Alternative I Master-Feeder Structure
Source: Created and reprinted by permission of Maury Cartine, JD, CPA.

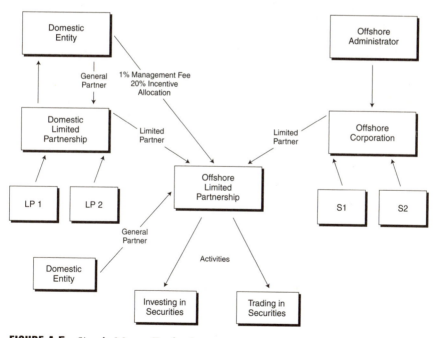

FIGURE A.5 Simple Master-Feeder Structure
Source: Created and reprinted by permission of Maury Cartine, JD, CPA.

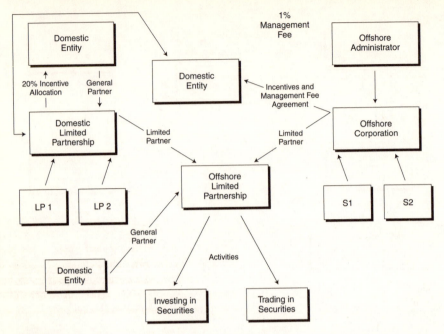

FIGURE A.6 Alternative I Master-Feeder Structure
Source: Created and reprinted by permission of Maury Cartine, JD, CPA.

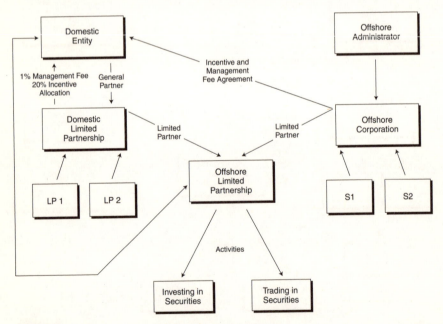

FIGURE A.7 Alternative II Master-Feeder Structure
Source: Created and reprinted by permission of Maury Cartine, JD, CPA.

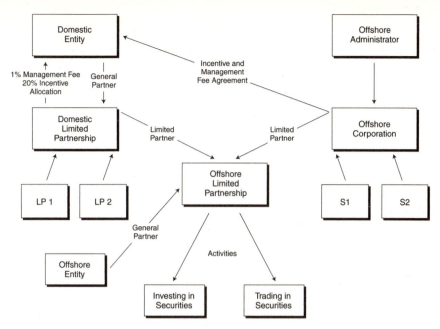

FIGURE A.8   Alternative III Master-Feeder Structure
Source: Created and reprinted by permission of Maury Cartine, JD, CPA.

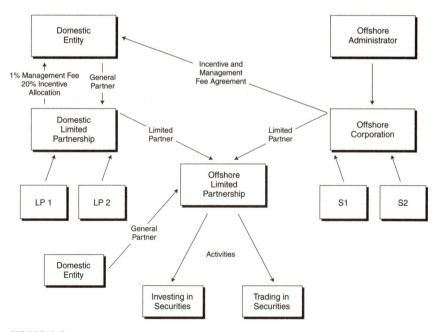

FIGURE A.9   Alternative IV Master-Feeder Structure
Source: Created and reprinted by permission of Maury Cartine, JD, CPA.

Resource Guide

Following is a list of service providers that can help you with most aspects of your business. The list has been gathered from a number of industry Web sites, publications, and personal contacts I have made over the years. Under no circumstances should you believe that I am endorsing any firm listed here or vouching for its ability to provide you with the services you need. This list should be used solely as a guide to service providers who may prove useful to you in building your business.

Prime Brokers

Bank of America Securities LLC
9 West 57th Street, 31st Floor
New York, NY 10019
(212) 583–8000

Barclays Capital Prime Services
200 Park Avenue, Floor 6
New York, NY 10166
(212) 412–2180

Bear Stearns Securities
583 Madison Ave.
New York, NY 10179
(212) 272–2000

Citigroup Global Prime Brokerage
390 Greenwich Street, 5th Floor
New York, NY 10013
(212) 723–4813

Credit Suisse
11 Madison Avenue
New York, NY 10010
(212) 325–6527

Fidelity Prime Services
World Trade Center
200 Seaport Boulevard
Boston, MA 02210
(800) 988–4794

Goldman Sachs
One New York Plaza, 44th Floor
New York, NY 10004
(212) 902–2938

Grace Financial Group
340 Old Country Road
Suite 102
Garden City, NY 11530
(516) 240-8195

Jefferies & Co.
520 Madison Avenue, 12th Floor
New York, NY 10022
(212) 707–6492

UBS HedgeFund Services
1285 Avenue of the Americas
New York, NY 10019
(800) 838–6096

VanthedgePoint Group, Inc.
61 Broadway
Suite 1915
New York, NY 10006
(212) 514-8639

Lawyers

Akin, Gump, Strauss, Hauer & Feld
590 Madison Avenue, 20th Floor
New York, NY 10022
(212) 872–1030

Arnold & Porter LLP
399 Park Avenue, 38th Floor
New York, NY 10022–4690
(212) 715–1000

Cobb & Eisenberg LLC
329 Riverside Avenue
Westport, CT 06880
(203) 222–1940

Davis Graham & Stubbs LLP
1550 Seventeenth Street, Suite 500
Denver, CO 80202
(303) 892–9400

Dechert LLP
30 Rockefeller Plaza, 23rd Floor
New York, NY 10112–2200
(212) 698–3500

Goodwin Procter LLP
Exchange Place
53 State Street
Boston, MA 02109
(617) 570–1559

Herrick, Feinstein LLP
2 Park Avenue, 21st Floor
New York, NY 10016
(212) 592–1558

Katten Muchin Rosenman LLP
575 Madison Avenue, 11th Floor
New York, NY 10022–2585
(212) 940–8930

Kirkpatrick & Lockhart Nicholson Graham LLP
State Street Financial Center
One Lincoln Street
Boston, MA 02111–2950
(617) 261–3208

Lowenstein Sandler PC
65 Livingston Avenue
Roseland, NJ 07068–1791
(973) 597–2424

Orrick
666 Fifth Avenue, 21st Floor
New York, NY 10103–0001
(212) 506–5000

Sadis & Golberg
551 Fifth Avenue, 21st Floor
New York, NY 10176
(212) 947–3793

Schulte Roth & Zabel
919 Third Avenue
New York, NY 10022
(212) 756–2567

Seward & Kissel
One Battery Park Plaza, 21st Floor
New York, NY 10004
(212) 574–1231

Stroock & Stroock & Lavan
180 Maiden Lane
New York, NY 10038–4982
(212) 806–5400

Tannenbaum Helpern Syracuse & Hirschtritt LLP
900 Third Avenue
New York, NY 10022
(212) 508–6700

Walkers
Walkers House
P.O. Box 265GT
Mary Street
George Town, Grand Cayman
(345) 914–4223

Administrators

Bank of Butterfield/Butterfield Fund Services
P.O. Box HM 195
Hamilton, Bermuda
HMAX
(441) 299–3954

BISYS
105 Eisenhower Parkway
Roseland, NJ 07068
(973) 461–2500

BNY Alternative Investment Services
One Wall Street, 42nd Floor
New York, NY 10286
(212) 495–1784

Fortis Prime Fund Solutions
153 East 53rd Street, 27th Floor
New York, NY 10022
(212) 340–5545

HSBC Alternative Fund Services
330 Madison Avenue, 5th Floor
New York, NY 10017
(212) 715–6491

Olympia Capital Management LP
295 Madison Avenue, 5th Floor
New York, NY 10017
(212) 403–9526

PFPC Trust Company
301 Bellevue Parkway
Wilmington, DE 19809
(302) 791–2000

Price Meadows
11747 NE First Street
Bellevue, WA 98005
(425) 454–3770

Spectrum Global Fund Services
200 North LaSalle Street
Chicago, IL 60601
(312) 697–9900

Accountants

Anchin, Block & Anchin LLP
1375 Broadway, 18th Floor
New York, NY 10018
(212) 840–3456

BDO Seidman LLP
330 Madison Avenue, 4th Floor
New York, NY 10017
(212) 885–8505

Coleman, Epstein, Berlin & Company LLP
515 North State Street, Suite 2300
Chicago, IL 60610
(312) 245–0077

Deloitte & Touche
1633 Broadway
New York, NY 10019
(212) 492–4800

Eisner LLP
750 Third Avenue, 16th Floor
New York, NY 10017–2703
(212) 891–4062

Ernst & Young
5 Times Square
New York, NY 10036
(212) 773–2252

Goldstein Golub Kessler LLP
1185 Avenue of the Americas, Suite 500
New York, NY 10036–2602
(212) 372–1535

Grant Thornton LLP
60 Broad Street, 25th Floor
New York, NY 10004
(212) 422–1000

Halpern & Associates, LLC
143 Weston Road
Weston, CT 06883
(203) 227–0313

KPMG LLP
345 Park Avenue
New York, NY 10154
(212) 758–9700

PricewaterhouseCoopers
300 Madison Avenue
New York, NY 10017
(646) 471–7830

Rothstein Kass
1350 Avenue of the Americas, 15th Floor
New York, NY 10019
(212) 997–0500

Notes

Chapter 1

1. Amanda Cantrell, "Hedge funds launch, close in record numbers" (March 2006). Retrieved August 8, 2006, from http://money.cnn.com/2006/03/01/markets/hedgefund_stats/index.htm.
2. Deborah Stead (ed.), "Up Front: For Hedge Funds, Some Sweet Deals" (May 8, 2006). Retrieved August 11, 2006, from Frontline—Betting on the Market—Pros Peter Lynch: http://www.pbs.org/wgbh/pages/frontline/shows/betting/pros/lynch.html.
3. Reprinted from the March 1949 issue of *Fortune* by special permission. ©1949 Time Inc. All rights reserved.
4. United States Securities and Exchange Commission, "Implications of the growth of hedge funds: Staff report to the United States Securities and Exchange Commission" (September 2003). Retrieved August 8, 2006 from http://www.sec.gov/news/studies/hedgefunds0903.pdf.
5. John Thackray, "Whatever happened to the hedge funds?" *Institutional Investor* (May 1977): 70–73.
6. U.S. Securities and Exchange Commission, "Accredited investors" (July 2000). Retrieved August 8, 2006, from http://www.sec.gov/answers/accred.htm.
7. GPO Access, United States Code, 2000 Edition. Title 15, Chapter 2D, Subchapter 1, Sec. 80a-2. Retrieved August 8, 2006, from http://frwebgate.access.gpo.gov/cgi-bin/getdoc.cgi?dbname=browse_usc&docid=Cite:+15USC80a-2.
8. Royal Vegas Poker, "The History of Poker." Retrieved August 8, 2006, from http://www.royalvegaspoker.com/history-of-Poker.asp?BTag=ad_157206.
9. E-zine Articles, "History of Texas Hold'em." Retrieved August 8, 2006, from http://ezinearticles.com/?History-of-Texas-Hold-em&id=205439.
10. Ibid.
11. This includes the legal work for the documents and all setup fees for the entities, but does not include infrastructure costs and/or investment assets.
12. Jesse Eisinger, "A David toppled hedge fund rule, but was Goliath really so bad?" *Wall Street Journal* (July 28, 2006), C1.
13. United States General Accounting Office. "Testimony before the subcommittee on government efficiency and financial management, Committee on Government Reform, House of Representatives: Securities and Exchange Commission—Preliminary observations on SEC's spending and strategic planning" (July 23, 2003). Retrieved August 8, 2006, from http://www.gao.gov/new.items/d03969t.pdf.

14. Van Hedge Fund Advisors International, LLC. "Size of Hedge Fund Universe." Retrieved from http://www.hedgefund.com/abouthfs/universe/universe.htm.
15. Daniel Strachman, *Getting Started in Hedge Funds,* 2e. (Hoboken, N.J.: John Wiley & Sons, Inc., 2005.)

Chapter 2

1. This is just a ballpark figure on the legal fees. Other costs go into the set, and the fees range from lawyer to lawyer.
2. Jonathan Burton, "SEC proposes tighter 'softer dollar' rules: Use of commissions for investment research under fire," *MarketWatch* (October 20, 2005). Retrieved August 9, 2006, from http://www.marketwatch.com/News/Story/Story.aspx?guid=%7B373BBC75-B693-457F-B656-A540F21CC034%7D.

Chapter 3

1. "Berger & Montague, P.C. Client Files Class Action Against Bayou Hedge Fund Entities, Citibank, Hennessee Group, Sterling Stamos Capital Management and Others on Behalf of Bayou Hedge Fund Investors," *Market Wire* (November 2005). Retrieved August 11, 2006, from http://findarticles.com/p/articles/mi_pwwi/is_200511/ai_n15850332.
2. Amanda Cantrell, "Bayou Founder, CFO Plead Guilty to Fraud," CNN (September 29, 2005). Retrieved August 11, 2006, from http://money.cnn.com/2005/09/29/markets/bayou/index.htm.
3. "Berger & Montague, P.C. Client Files Class Action Against Bayou Hedge Fund Entities, Citibank, Hennessee Group, Sterling Stamos Capital Management and Others on Behalf of Bayou Hedge Fund Investors," *Market Wire* (November 2005). Retrieved August 11, 2006, from http://findarticles.com/p/articles/mi_pwwi/is_200511/ai_n15850332.
4. United States District Court, District of Connecticut, Civil Action No.–Class Action Complaint: 305CV176 2. Retrieved August 11, 2006, from http://securities.stanford.edu/1035/BHFE05_01/20051117_f01c_0501762.pdf.
5. Securities and Exchange Commission, 17 CFR Part 230–Releases No. 33–8041; File No. S7–23–01, "Defining the Term 'Qualified Purchaser' under the Securities Act of 1933." Retrieved August 11, 2006, from http://www.sec.gov/rules/proposed/33–8041.htm.
6. University of Cincinnati College of Law, Security Lawyer's Deskbook, "The Investment Company Act of 1940." Retrieved August 17, 2006, from http://www.law.uc.edu/CCL/InvCoAct/sec3.html.
7. HR 3162: Uniting and Strengthening America by Providing Appropriate Tools Required to Intercept and Obstruct Terrorism (USA Patriot Act) Act of 2001 (Enrolled as Agreed to or Passed by Both House and Senate). Section 326. Retrieved August 11, 2006, from http://thomas.loc.gov/cgi-bin/query/D?c107:4:./temp/~c1076T6dS4.
8. Ibid., Section 352.

9. Ibid.
10. Ibid.
11. Ibid., Section 326.

Chapter 4

1. Steven Felsenstein, Joel Telpner, and Brenda Chavez, Greenberg Traurig Alert: "New NASD Rule 2790 Revises Retrictions on the Purchase and Sales of Initial Public Offerings" (January 2004). Retrieved August 11, 2006, from http://www.gtlaw.com/pub/alerts/2004/felsensteins_01.pdf.
2. Ibid.
3. "Hedge Fund Accounting Basics." Copyright 2001–2006 Fund-Investors, LLC, http://www.hedgefundcenter.com/wrapper.cfm?article_type=basics.
4. "Global Hedge Funds: Maze—Navigate the maze of opportunities" PFPC Worldwide Inc. Copyright 2004. http://www.pfpc.com/pdfs/BRO_Hedge_Fund.pdf.
5. Ibid.
6. Ibid.
7. Ibid.
8. Australian Stock Exchange Website Glossary, http://www.asx.com.au/investor/lmi/how/AbsoluteFundsGlossary.htm.
9. Texas MBD Hedge Fund Organization—McCombs School of Business Website Glossary of Terms, http://www.mccombs.utexas.edu/students/MBAHFO/glossary.asp#H.
10. Nandita Das, Richard Kish, David L. Muething, Larry W. Traylor, "An Overview of the Hedge Fund Industry," Martindale Center for the Study of Private Enterprise, Lehigh University 2002 Series 1, http://www.lehigh.edu/~incntr/publications/2002_series_1.pdf.
11. Ibid.
12. Antoine Bernheim, "Repeal of the Ten Commandments: The Impact on the offshore hedge fund administrations industry," http://www.hedgefundnews.com/news_n_info/article_detail.php?id=260.
13. Dermot S. Butler, "How to Select an Administrator: Due Diligence or What to Look For—What to Ask." Delivered at AIMA and Euronext 7th Annual Investor Forum, September 25, 2002, http://www.customhousegroup.com/How%20to%20Select%20Admin.htm.

Chapter 5

1. Maury Cartine, CPA, "Unrelated Business Taxable Income" BISYS Alternative Investment Services (Fall 2006).
2. Ibid.
3. Ibid.
4. "Global Hedge Funds: Maze—Navigate the maze of opportunities" PFPC Worldwide Inc. Copyright 2004. http://www.pfpc.com/pdfs/BRO_Hedge_Fund.pdf.

Chapter 6

1. FBI History: Famous Case: Willie Sutton. Retrieved August 11, 2006, from http://www.fbi.gov/libref/historic/famcases/sutton/sutton.htm.
2. Frontline—Betting on the Market—Pros Peter Lynch, http://www.pbs.org/wgbh/pages/frontline/shows/betting/pros/lynch.html.

Chapter 7

1. Daniel A. Strachman, *Julian Robertson: A Tiger in the Land of Bulls and Bears* (New York: John Wiley & Sons, Inc., 2004).

Chapter 9

1. Stanley Weiser and Oliver Stone, "Wall Street" 1987—Third Draft April 23, 1987, http://sfy.ru/sfy.html?script=wall_street.

Glossary

Absolute-return fund A fund that attempts to perform positively for investors regardless of market conditions. An absolute-return fund is not benchmarked against traditional long-only indices because it is able to go long and short to provide returns to investors.

Accredited investor Rule 501 or Regulation D of the Securities Act of 1933 defines an "accredited investor" as any of the following:

1. A bank, insurance company, registered investment company, business development company, or small business investment company
2. An employee benefit plan, within the meaning of the Employee Retirement Income Security Act, if a bank, insurance company, or registered investment adviser makes the investment decisions, or if the plan has total assets in excess of $5 million
3. A charitable organization, corporation, or partnership with assets exceeding $5 million
4. A director, executive officer, or general partner of the company selling the securities
5. A business in which all the equity owners are accredited investors
6. A natural person who has individual net worth, or joint net worth with the person's spouse, that exceeds $1 million at the time of the purchase
7. A natural person with income exceeding $200,000 in each of the two most recent years or joint income with a spouse exceeding $300,000 for those years and a reasonable expectation of the same income level in the current year
8. A trust with assets in excess of $5 million, not formed to acquire the securities offered, whose purchases a sophisticated person makes

Administrator A service provider hired by a hedge fund to calculate performance and net asset value for the fund and to perform other record-keeping functions.

Alpha The return as measured by the fund's performance over the risk-free rate and/or other performance measurement tools, including but not limited to traditional and nontraditional indices.

Alternative assets Any investment vehicle that is not considered a traditional or long-only fund. Alternative assets include hedge funds, private equity funds, and commodities pools that are not regulated under the Securities Act of 1940.

Annual rate of return The compounded gain or loss in a fund's net asset value during a calendar year.

Arbitrage   An investment strategy that takes advantage of the mispricing of securities from one market to another.

Assets under management   Includes all investments, leveraged and unleveraged, including cash, that are overseen by a fund manager.

Average annual return (annualized rate of return)   Cumulative compounded gains and losses divided by the number of years of a fund's existence.

Average monthly return   Cumulative gains and losses divided by the number of months of the investment's life, with compounding taken into account.

Average rate of return   The investment's performance or lack of performance over a specific period of time.

Back-test   The use of historical data to prove or disprove a specific trading methodology.

Bear market   Prolonged period of falling prices.*

Bull market   Prolonged period of rising prices.*

Clearing   The process of reconciling transactions between the manager and the broker once a trade is entered and executed.

Commodity trading advisor (CTA)   A person or entity providing advice to others on investments in commodity futures, options, and foreign-exchange contracts.

Custodian   A bank, trust company, or other financial institution that holds and protects a fund's assets and provides other services, including collecting money from investors, distributing redemption proceeds, and maintaining margin accounts.

Derivatives   Securities that take their values from other securities.

Diversification   The variety of investments in a fund's portfolio. In diversification, risk-averse fund managers combine investments that are unlikely to all move in the same direction at the same time.

Drawdown   The amount of loss that an investment experiences from its highest value to its lowest value. The investment's maximum drawdown over a specific period of time is often used in a way to determine the risk associated with the investment.

Due diligence   Questions by investors to the manager regarding investment style and strategy as well as the manager's background and track record.*

Exposure   The extent to which an investment has the potential to change based on changes in market conditions. In the hedge fund world, exposure is measured on a net basis. Net exposure takes into account the difference between the long positions versus the short positions. For example, if a fund is 150 percent long and 65 percent short, its net exposure would be 85 percent.

Fair value   The price at which a single unit of a security would trade between parties that don't have interests in the issue.

Forward contract   A private, over-the-counter derivative instrument that requires one party to sell and another party to buy a specific security or commodity at a preset price on an agreed-upon date in the future.

---

*Strachman, D. *Getting Started in Hedge Funds, Second Ed.* (Hoboken, N.J.: John Wiley & Sons, 2005).

Fund of funds   An investment vehicle that invests in other hedge funds or other investment vehicles.

Futures contract   An agreement to buy or sell a commodity or security at an agreed-upon date in the future.

General partner   The individual or firm that operates, develops, and runs a limited partnership.

High-water mark   An agreement in the offering document that provides for the manager to earn an incentive fee on profits only after the fund's performance surpasses its highest net asset value from the prior period.

Hurdle rate   A set return rate that the fund must achieve before the fund manager collects his or her performance fee. The hurdle rate is usually a fixed rate such as LIBOR or the one-year Treasury bill rate plus a fixed amount of basis points.

Incentive fee (performance fee)   The fee, usually 20 percent, that a fund manager is paid on the profits made in the portfolio.

Inception date   The day on which a fund starts trading.

Limited liability company   A legal structure that is the hedge fund investment vehicle.*

Limited partnership   A legal structure that is used as a hedge fund vehicle.*

Liquidity   The ease with which an investment can be sold without impacting its price in the market.

Lockup   The term during which an investor must maintain his or her investment in the fund (i.e., a period during which he or she is not allowed to redeem assets).

Long position   A transaction to purchase shares of stock resulting in a net positive position.*

Management fee   The charge that a fund manager assesses to investors, often used to cover operating expenses. The annual fee generally ranges from 0.5 to 2 percent of an investor's entire holdings in the fund and is usually collected on a quarterly basis.

Margin call   Demand that an investor deposit enough money or securities to bring a margin account up to the minimum maintenance requirements.*

Minimum investment   The smallest amount that an investor is permitted contribute to a hedge fund as an initial investment. Minimum investment requirements can range from $50,000 to $5 million, but most funds insist on $500,000 to $1 million.

Net asset value (NAV)   The market value of a fund's total assets.

Offshore fund   An investment vehicle that is set up outside of the United States.

Onshore fund   An investment vehicle that is set up in the United States that is available to U.S. citizens.*

Option   A contract that gives parties the right to buy or sell a specific asset or security at a specified strike price by a preset date.

---

*Strachman, D. *Getting Started in Hedge Funds, Second Ed.* (Hoboken, N.J.: John Wiley & Sons, 2005).

Performance fee   Fee paid to manager based on how well the investment strategy performs.*

Portfolio manager   A company or individual that manages the firm's assets.

Poison pill   Any number of legal defensive tactics written into a corporate charter to fend off the advances of an unwanted suitor.*

Prime broker   A securities firm that provides hedge funds with operational services, including trading, reporting, and financing.

Private-equity fund   A fund that makes investment in companies that are not yet public.

Private placement memorandum   The documents that set forth the hedge fund offering. These detail how the fund is operated, its management, its risks, and its potential for reward.

Quantitative analysis   Security analysis that uses objective statistical information to determine when to buy and sell securities.*

Redemption   The sale of all an investor's interests in the fund.

Redemption fee   A fee imposed by hedge fund managers at the time the investor redeems his or her investment.

Redemption notice period   The notice that an investor must provide to the hedge fund manager before withdrawing his or her investment from the fund.

Section 3(c)(1)   A provision in the Investment Company Act of 1940 that allows certain hedge funds to be established without registering as investment advisers, provided their shares are owned by no more than 100 investors.

Section 3(c)(7)   A provision in the Investment Company Act of 1940 that allows hedge funds to have more than 100 investors, provided all investors are considered to be qualified purchasers.

Sharpe ratio   The ratio of return above the minimum acceptable return divided by the standard deviation. It provides information of the return per unit of dispersion risk.*

Short position   A transaction to sell shares of stock that the investor does not own.*

Short sales   The process of borrowing securities from a broker and "selling them into the market" with the belief that the security can be bought back at a later date at a lower price.

Spread   The difference in price or yield between two securities.

Standard deviation   A measure of the dispersion of a group of numerical values from the mean. It is calculated by taking the difference between each number in the group and the arithmetic average, squaring them to give the variance, summing them, and taking the square root.*

Traditional investments   Products whose performances are correlated with broad stock market or fixed-income market.

---

*Strachman, D. *Getting Started in Hedge Funds, Second Ed.* (Hoboken, N.J.: John Wiley & Sons, 2005).

Glossary Sources

Global Value Investing: http://www.numeraire.com/margin.htm

Hedge Fund Alert Glossary: http://www.hfalert.com/NewPages/Index.cfm?Article_ID=61250

The Free Dictionary by Farlex: http://www.thefreedictionary.com/Hedge+funds

Venture Japan. Hedge Fund Glossary of Terms: http://www.venturejapan.com/index.htm

Bibliography

Australian Stock Exchange Website Glossary. Retrieved August 11, 2006, from http://www.asx.com.au/investor/lmi/how/AbsoluteFundsGlossary.htm.

Berger & Montague, P.C. Client Files Class Action Against Bayou Hedge Fund Entities, Citibank, Hennessee Group, Sterling Stamos Capital Management and Others on Behalf of Bayou Hedge Fund Investors," *Market Wire* (November 2005). Retrieved August 11, 2006, from http://findarticles.com/p/articles/mi_pwwi/is_200511/ai_n15850332.

Bernheim, A. "Repeal of the Ten Commandments: The Impact on the offshore hedge fund administrations industry." Retrieved August 11, 2006, from http://www.hedgefundnews.com/news_n_info/article_detail.php?id=260.

Burton, J. "SEC proposes tighter 'softer dollar' rules: Use of commissions for investment research under fire." *MarketWatch* (October 20, 2005). Retrieved August 9, 2006, from http://www.marketwatch.com/News/Story/Story.aspx?guid=%7B373BBC75-B693–457F-B656-A540F21CC034%7D.

Butler, D. S. "How to Select an Administrator: Due Diligence: What to Look For—What to Ask." Delivered at AIMA and Euronext 7th Annual Investor Forum, September 25, 2002. Retrieved August 11, 2006, from http://www.customhousegroup.com/How%20to%20Select%20Admin.htm.

Cantrell, A. "Bayou Founder, CFO Plead Guilty to Fraud," CNN (September 29, 2005). Retrieved August 11, 2006, from http://money.cnn.com/2005/09/29/markets/bayou/index.htm.

————. "Hedge funds launch, close in record numbers" (March 2006). Retrieved August 8, 2006, from http://money.cnn.com/2006/03/01/markets/hedgefund_stats/index.htm.

Cartine, M. "Unrelated Business Taxable Income." BISYS Alternative Investment Services (Fall 2006).

Das, N., R. Kish, D. L. Muething, and L. W. Traylor. "An Overview of the Hedge Fund Industry." Martindale Center for the Study of Private Enterprise, Lehigh University 2002 Series 1. Retrieved August 11, 2006, from http://www.lehigh.edu/~incntr/publications/2002_series_1.pdf.

Eisinger, J. "A David toppled hedge fund rule, but was Goliath really so bad?" *Wall Street Journal* (July 28, 2006), C1.

E-zine Articles. "History of Texas Hold'em." Retrieved August 8, 2006, from http://ezinearticles.com/?History-of-Texas-Hold-em&id=205439.

Felsenstein, S., J. Telpner, and B. Chavez. Greenberg Traurig Alert: "New NASD Rule 2790 Revises Retrictions on the Purchase and Sales of Initial Public Offerings"

(January 2004). Retrieved August 11, 2006, from http://www.gtlaw.com/pub/alerts/2004/felsensteins_01.pdf.

FBI History: Famous Case: Willie Sutton. Retrieved August 11, 2006, from http://www.fbi.gov/libref/historic/famcases/sutton/sutton.htm.

Frontline: Betting on the Market. Pros: Peter Lynch. Retrieved August 11, 2006, from http://www.pbs.org/wgbh/pages/frontline/shows/betting/pros/lynch.html.

Fund Investors, LLC. "Hedge Fund Accounting Basics." Copyright 2001–2006. Retrieved August 11, 2006, from http://www.hedgefundcenter.com/wrapper .cfm?article_type=basics.

GPO Access: United States Code, 2000 Edition. Title 15, Chapter 2D, Subchapter 1, Sec. 80a-2. Retrieved August 8, 2006, from http://frwebgate.access.gpo .gov/cgi-bin/getdoc.cgi?dbname=browse_usc&docid=Cite:+15USC80a-2.

HR 3162: Uniting and Strengthening America by Providing Appropriate Tools Required to Intercept and Obstruct Terrorism (USA Patriot Act) Act of 2001 (Enrolled as Agreed to or Passed by Both House and Senate). Sections 326 & 352. Retrieved August 11, 2006, from http://thomas.loc.gov/cgi-bin/query/ D?c107:4:./temp/~c1076T6dS4.

PFPC Worldwide Inc. "Global Hedge Funds: Maze—Navigate the maze of opportunities." Copyright 2004. Retrieved August 11, 2006, from http://www.pfpc .com/pdfs/BRO_Hedge_Fund.pdf.

Royal Vegas Poker. "The History of Poker." Retrieved August 8, 2006, from http://www.royalvegaspoker.com/history-of-Poker.asp?BTag=ad_157206.

Stead, D. (ed.). "Up Front: For Hedge Funds, Some Sweet Deals" (May 8, 2006). Retrieved August 11, 2006, from Frontline—Betting on the Market—Pros Peter Lynch: http://www.pbs.org/wgbh/pages/frontline/shows/betting/pros/lynch.html.

Strachman, D. *Getting Started in Hedge Funds,* Second Ed. (Hoboken, N.J.: John Wiley & Sons, Inc., 2005.)

Strachman, D. *Julian Robertson: A Tiger in the Land of Bulls and Bears.* (New York: John Wiley & Sons, Inc., 2004.)

Texas MBD Hedge Fund Organization: McCombs School of Business Website Glossary of Terms. Retrieved August 11, 2006, from http://www.mccombs.utexas .edu/students/MBAHFO/glossary.asp#H.

Thackray, J. "Whatever happened to the hedge funds?" *Institutional Investor* (1977 May): 70–73.

United States District Court, District of Connecticut, Civil Action No.–Class Action Complaint 305CV176 2. Retrieved August 11, 2006, from http://securities .stanford.edu/1035/BHFE05_01/20051117_f01c_0501762.pdf.

United States General Accounting Office. "Testimony before the subcommittee on government efficiency and financial management, Committee on Government Reform, House of Representatives: Securities and Exchange Commission— Preliminary observations on SEC's spending and strategic planning" (July 23, 2003). Retrieved August 8, 2006, from http://www.gao.gov/new.items/d03969t .pdf.

United States Securities and Exchange Commission, 17 CFR Part 230–Releases No. 33–8041; File No. S7–23–01. "Defining the Term 'Qualified Purchaser' under

the Securities Act of 1933." Retrieved August 11, 2006, from http://www.sec
.gov/rules/proposed/33–8041.htm.

United States Securities and Exchange Commission. "Accredited investors" (July
2000). Retrieved August 8, 2006, from http://www.sec.gov/answers/accred.htm.

United States Securities and Exchange Commission. "Implications of the growth of
hedge funds: Staff report to the United States Securities and Exchange Commission" (September 2003). Retrieved August 8, 2006, from http://www.sec.gov/
news/studies/hedgefunds0903.pdf.

University of Cincinnati College of Law. Security Lawyer's Deskbook. "The Investment Company Act of 1940." Retrieved August 17, 2006, from http://www.law
.uc.edu/CCL/InvCoAct/sec3.html.

Van Hedge Fund Advisors International, LLC. "Size of Hedge Fund Universe." Retrieved from http://www.hedgefund.com/abouthfs/universe/universe.htm.

The Strachman Report – The Newsletter for Investors That
Cuts Through The Noise.

The **Strachman Report** is a new, exciting and informative bi-monthly newsletter with a distinctive viewpoint for investors. Published by Daniel Strachman, a leading author and commentator on money management, The Strachman Report cuts through the clutter to provide valuable information and insights that will help hedge fund and mutual fund investors meet their long-term financial goals. In the pages of The Strachman Report you'll find stories you won't find anywhere else. You'll get insightful, provocative stories and market commentary that separates the wheat from the vast chaff choking most market coverage. The editorial mission is based upon a simple investing principle: Don't pick the fund; pick the fund manager. The Strachman Report is a must-read for investors with a sophisticated view of the markets and a passion for investing.

Cut Here
